It's Your World

This book is dedicated to the moon. All words rose before the sun and awoke under your watch. The early morning skies hushed as we wrote. In the dark we danced with possibilities. Your whispers led the way while your light sounded the rhythms. Then the day would come we'd bid farewell. The days would often be filled with light and joy, but I longed for the night. For in the sun I would play, but I only danced with the moon.

I wrote this book for this one moment… just now, the beginning. The beginning is the most important part, here in the possibility.

My road is much like yours. Our tracks may have diverged but our origins are the same.
We came with warm hearts and open hands. We looked for connection and longed to be close.

Life was simple, days were fresh. We had no past, there was only today. But then one day the future came knocking. We had to answer.

So, we donned masks and went to the masquerade. Here we played pretend and hid what was true. Schooled to not think and shamed should we feel. Much of what was natural, lost to what was appropriate.

Time took our acts, pulled them into habits then weaved them into patterns. The endless pieces of pleasure and pain became our personal mosaic. When we live the same pattern over and over, the same day over and over, it becomes us. It becomes our personality, our character.

But life cannot thrive in rigid patterns. Rigidity is the dawn of disease. For all life is soft in birth and hard in death. When life becomes rigid, it begins to die. If we don't break these ancient patterns, they will break us.

I have spent much of my time in my clinical practice removing masks and helping people bend instead of break. I hear many stories, but I listen to the storyteller. Looking for the dancer in the dance, the story within the story. Just stillness and simple listening. For the greatest therapeutic tool is a clear reflection.

When people stop…take a look, they get a clear view of where they are. It is amazing when lamps are lit how much we can see.

The truth is when we understand our own pain, we can understand others. It is what the world is waiting for. There's an old saying in

Buddhism. 'If you know you, you know the person beside you. If you know the place around you, you know the world.' For our beacons may be different but the light is the same.

This book is a conversation through life. It is about the patterns that ignite pain and ways to douse the fires. It is about returning to the garden and playing in fields of possibility.

I wrote this for you. I wrote this for me. We can have great perspectives, clinging to hopes and certainties, but chains of habit are not easily broken. Perspectives will blur, chains will bind and whatever we cling to will be lost.

This book is a reminder of who you are. A reminder you are loved. A reminder of your potentiality. A reminder the dance is short but the music is left unbroken.

I wrote because I don't like the way we live. I know many of us have good lives but there's something about it that I do not like. I don't like that some feel anxious. I don't like that some feel lonely. I don't like that some don't feel at all. I don't like that today 17,000 children will die of hunger. All of this is connected, one suffers we all suffer.

But where there's ruin there is also fortune. For the liberation of one is the liberation of all

In my 20 years of listening and conversing with patients, I would say something or hear something that cracked a vicious cycle or dented a rigid pattern, so I wrote it down. This book is an accumulation of the very best of those conversations.

Read this book with your eyes, read with your mind but mostly read with your heart. For to touch the soul, we must open all the windows.

If the words are to be of use they must be strong words. The ones that blow past our habitual reactions and find their way to our center. If these words don't reach the place where emotions rise then it is only information, not knowledge.

A great journey without a guide could be endless. I have chosen grandmother or she chose me. Throughout many cultures grand-mother is the wise one, the truest mirror, the clearest reflection. She will be our guide.

I didn't want to stop writing this book. To be around grandmother gave me a quiet solace. I will try to read this book every day the rest of my life. It recalls me to the heart, it reminds me to feel.

Our society seduces us with numbing agents, if we don't push back we get pulled in. Each morning like today, I will pick up this book and read. Just read anything, anywhere.
Grandmother is a great reminder of the truth. I don't trust many minds, but hers I do.

This book carries the echoes of Rumi, Lao Tzu and many other great teachers from the past. Let their words remind you of what you al-ready know. We only need to unwind what has been wound. For the only thing to learn is to learn how to unlearn.

I have chosen to write in poetic form. For all great ceremonies around birth, death and marriage call upon poetry. Hailing words to slip past the guards and pierce the heart.
Perhaps it was just simpler for me. Poetry allowed me to use one word instead of two. We can take great liberties, screw up and then call it poetry.

My intent is not vital, what is important is your perception. Let us shun the shoulds and avoid the webs of wrong or right.

This book is not a fix, for nothing is broken. It is not advice, for you've heard enough.
It will not tell you what to do or make the hard stuff go away.
It will remind you of you. All of you.

This book shall the call the warrior, spark the lover, strengthen the peacemaker, inspire the alchemist and hail the wizard.

I see many clients in my practice. I continue to learn and continue to listen.
I often feel I should just give them the book. I get clouded, but grandmother doesn't.

She is fluid as the wind and deep as the sea. She dances with the sun and whispers to the moon. The quieter I become the more she speaks. When I'm really still there are moments I swear I can hear her voice.

Let yourself go. Let us embrace the dark and begin in the twilight. Let grandmother lead the way. She's been listening and has been waiting for you. Come, take a rest. Let her carry the load, she knows the way.

She sat in her favorite chair. She always sat so quiet and still. Her eyes gazing out her window, her hands resting on her lap. She did not need much, wanted very little. Contentment was her greatest treasure, peace her closest friend. It was in the way she talked and in her walk. There was no mask, she didn't need a disguise. It was her world. She was profound and she was subtle. She was my teacher. She was my friend.
Her mind clear as the ocean.
Her body strong as the oak.
Her spirit bright as the sun.
The elements so mixed in her, that nature did bend and bow.
Often, I sat with her. Sat for hours. She was the moon in my darkest nights. Sometimes we talked, she mostly listened. She let me talk away my clouds. When she spoke she did not mince her words. They were sharp daggers tearing away the cloak of my distress. Through the years, we cut away hordes of senseless noise. She showed me the ways of the wind, the aimlessness of the breeze and the purpose of a gust. We waded through waves of my darkness. She braced me as the fears crashed upon my shores. Held my hand as I sunk to the bottom. There we sat. No rush to rise. For even there she was here. She was the light that broke through the murk and pulled me to climb.
From the depths of stillness, I rose. I followed the light. I followed it to the sun. There we danced, we played.
She smiled me into smiling.
She talked me into talking.
She laughed me into laughing.
She taught me love.
She showed me life.

In my ninth year, the spring of life, our world is monkey bars and horse play. We run with the wind and tag the stars. We dance with daisies and fly like falcons. Sunny days sweeping the clouds away. We live where the air is sweet. Running beyond mothers eyes, far from her grasp. Years from the apple and miles from the asp. But life takes a turn and the falcon flies from the falconer. We stray from the meadows of play and run into competition. Playgrounds are now just a memory. In fields and gyms we gather. Captains choose sides. The strong begin to rule, the weak go quiet. We are all friends, all together, but we're being pulled into teams. Judged on skill, strength and skin. We learn to follow. Learn to battle. Learn war. The colors of the garden fade into black and white. Are you with us or against us? The right and the wrong. Who you are and where you belong. This is not our world, ours is kind and caring, we're just shocked and confused. Most go quietly. A few are taken. We feel the passing of something sweet, something wonderful. The air has lost a bit of its scent, the water its glitter and sky its color. We are children no longer. Closeness traded for contest and marbles for equipment. Play lost to sport.

Feelings are not had in this world. Hearts hush for survival. It is about winning. To show heart is to show weakness. So we don masks, carry disguises, learn to fit in, learn to survive.

This is it.

This is what happens.

The real world.

Yet the heart does not sleep, the spirit will not whither. They judge our bodies but can't crush our souls. For our world is just around the bend. The monkey bars are bare, the slides silent. But spring is calling. I can hear her echoes in the breeze. The soil needs tilling, the garden needs seeding. We must retake the playground, redeem our hearts, reclaim our world.

Grandmother: What's wrong my child?
Girl: I'm fine.
Gm: If you were fine I wouldn't ask.
G: I know. I know.
Gm: You know?
You always know
Always knowing is a sickness.
Give up knowing.
If you know, how will you ever grow?
If you know, how can you learn?
When you know you don't know,
you shall find your way.
If you wanna know, don't know.
G: Ok, ok.
I'm just stuck.
Gm: In what?
G: Like you say. I don't know.
Gm: If you're stuck, move!
G: It's not that simple.
Gm: Maybe it is.
G: What?
Gm: If it's cold make it hot.
If it's weak make it strong.
If you're stuck? Move
G: No. That's not it.
I think I'm depressed.
Gm: Depressed? That's a big word.
G: Well, I think I am.
Gm: Let me tell you about depression.

DEPRESSION

Nothing colder than the backwoods of depression.

Clouds fog the mind and
lurk through the body.
The harsh winds rise and
whirl you to the dark forest.
The smell of rot.

Slings and arrows of outrageous fortune.
The chill hardens the heart
and the dusk dissolves color,
Only shades of grey for even
the wounds are numb.

It is dark here
and still and dark
and cold and dark
and dark.

So very dark.

The warrior is lost
in a land of doubt.
To be or not?

They call it depression,
the bleakest indulgence.
Bearing whips and scorns of time.
The guards on high alert,
waiting for rain and shoes to drop.

Until you've been here
no one can explain
the pain, the drain.

Who cares.
Who cares!!!
Who cares?

I do.
You are not alone
You are good
You are loved
You, just the way you are.

Nothing to be ashamed of.
We all visit. We all fall.
The tangled wilderness
where travelers return.
It's not personal.
It was never personal.

Yes, this is in your head
and yes it's in your body
and yes it's in your soul.
These scars are far reaching.

You are not what happened to you.
Life happens.
It may seem big, it
may seem small.
It's not the event, but
the effect that matters.

I'm sorry it's gone this far.
I know you are tired.

Now you wait.
Wait for something to help,
for someone to get you,
for someone to save you.
To say or do that one thing
that will take it all away.

No one is coming.
I'm sorry.
They didn't come then,
they're not coming now.

Nobody can reach in that far.
Nobody can reach back that far.

It's a need frozen in time.
Waiting to be noticed, to be held, to be loved.
Left waiting.
You're still waiting.

You're searching through leaves,
what is only found in roots.
Dig a little deeper,
use both hands.

I know lightness can be lost
and darkness can be insatiable,
but no winter will last forever.
It's when you feel
you can't go on.
When it's so dark
you've lost yourself.
When you cannot bear
another minute...
move.

You must move.
Even if all you can do is crawl,
then crawl.

There is no bypass.
No breathing through it.
No wishing it away.
The only path out is the path in.
This road is not easy
but it is the way home.
It is the way of the heart.
Start moving the path will clear.

Open the windows,
free the dragons.

You are not your depression.
Depression is suppression.
Mountains of hurt,
capped and wrapped
in a cloak of numbness.
A hushed anger,
a chest caves,
the shoulders drop.
The soul draped and muffled.

Feel, you must feel, just feel.
For feelings are meant to be felt.
When you don't cry, you will lose why.
When you don't laugh, you will lose how.
When you don't rage, you will lose it.

Feelings are to be felt not followed.
I know this is not easy!
But look how far you've come.

How many times you fought
to get through the day.
I'm asking you to fight once more.
To fight for your life!
The Hun will rumble,
mountains will crumble.
The trees will shake,
the shen will wake.

Let it thunder
Shaking earth
Trembling sky!

When feelings move shades lift,
armors melt.
The windows to the sky open.
The sun strikes your face.
Wake, wake, wake..
The light is cracking through.
Great warriors know the sun,
it is their compass.
If you know your place with sky and star,
how could you be lost?

Morning has broken,
the sunshine warms your eyes.
A dream, all a dream, just a dream.
The birds are singing just for you.
A fresh dew on the flowers,
a crisp breeze blowing.
The backwoods are warming.
Don't go back to sleep, the
morning air is brimming with life.
Reclaim the name of action.
Now is the time.

Girl: That's depressing.
Grandmother: Exactly.
G: Ok maybe I'm not there.
Gm: Well, we all have a version of depression,
some of us just go deeper into the woods.
G: It's just hard at school.
Gm: Tell me. I'm listening.
G: Some kids are so mean. It's hard to watch.
Gm: Then don't just watch.
G: You mean run away?
Gm: No!!! Do something.
G: Like what?
Gm: Like anything! It's your world. Fight for justice.

JUSTICE

Love resides in the heart.
Justice inhabits our soul.

As a heart must love,
the soul must speak.
The judge that voices for
truth and right.

To observe injustice
and go quiet
is the great crime.
The road to the dark forest
is paved with this silence.

You were shocked,
you went quiet.
You were angry,
you went quiet.
Doubting mind,
you went quiet.
Doubting heart,
you went quiet.
The hush of toxicity
in a hell of complicity.

The reluctant witness.
Where eyes shut and ears closed.
The warrior hushed,
but what good is a warrior
if she's not willing to battle.
What good is a fighter
not willing to fight.
Is that the world you want?

In my world, this is not okay.
In my world, I will not go quiet.
In my world,
no one is less.
In my world,
all are equal.
In my world,
justice prevails.

I have always fought for my world.
Fight for yours.
Even if your voice shakes,
Fight.
Even if your knees weaken,
Fight.
Even if all are quiet,
Fight.

It's not about saving another.
We don't need heroes,
for there are no villains.
Our liberation is bound to each other.
It is not charity but unity.
Your oppression is my oppression.
Any injustice, for any being,
is woven through the seams that link
all life.
For personal growth has always
been married to societal progress.

They taught you to expect less,
but every time you expect less
your world becomes less.

For at times there is darkness.

Where the brightest of days
are flooded by dusk.
The trump will blast its futile horn.
Blowing hot air about the days of old.
Well, the good old days have gotten old.
Truly they are only good
because memory is so bad.

Yes, there will be struggle.
If you don't feel it
you're not listening.

For a game of chess is not won by
only moving forward.
Even in the coldest ofnights
the stars will flicker and the horizon
will be brimming with hope.
For life does not go backward
nor lingers in yesterday.

Yes bullies will bully. For a while
they seem unstoppable but throughout
time, tyrants always tumble.

Look in the mirror and get off the fence!
There are not good people on both sides.
The left is not right and the right has not left.
In fact there is only one side and the other
hawks oppression and breeds gluttony.

Do not be thrown into despair
for they are the ones lost in despair.
It is despair that would ignore the poor.
It is despair that would harm children.
It is despair that would hoard riches.

Do not let despair become a companion.

Don't look away,
the scales have been tipped.
Light the dark,
hear the unbearable,
see the unseeable.

Bang the gavel!
Order in the court!
The magistrate must speak.
The judge will right the wrongs.

The great civil action
will begin in people's minds.
If not now, then when?
If not you, then who?
For the great injustice is the hushed spirit,
the greatest crime is the silenced soul.
The stench of conformity,
the disease of being well adjusted.

Yes, speaking up has consequences,
so does silence.
Better to face music,
than quietly fade away.

Feel the outrage and be sick
of the cruelty.
There is a better world,
there must be.
For they may stomp on grass,
but they cannot stop
the coming of spring.

A heart void of love
will wither.
A soul void of justice
will torment.
Be surprised
Be curious
Be enraged
Be defiant
Just...
don't be quiet!
It's your world...
Fight for it!

Girl: It's my world?
Grandmother: Don't let them take it away. You create your world.
G: Then what is the real world?
Gm: Whatever world you choose, is the real world.
G: What are you talking about?
Gm: You are the creator. How you see the world becomes your world. Choose your world, then fight for it. If you believe the world is good, then you must act to create that. Make your inside your outside. This is harmony. Do you believe the world is good?
G: Yes. I think so.
Gm: Don't let them take it away. When we are young we see the world more simply. More as it is.
G: So, the world is good?
Gm: If you believe it to be, then it is.
G: At school they've been teasing this boy.
Gm: Why?
G: He's new.
Gm: New?
G: Fresh off the boat.
Gm: What an awful thing to say.
G: He is. His family just arrived on a boat.
Gm: Oh?
G: They say he's an immigrant. They tease him cus he's different.
Gm: Oh, I see. The greatest hate for the least reason. The face of racism.

RACISM

Behind the fragile veil of society
there is a prison.
The seediest institution.
Racism.

The dark toil under the sun,
while guards lay down the law.
The wardens sit and watch,
while kings count their money.

Do you see color?

The dark lords or the fair queens.
Where the light is good
and the night is bad.
From white lies to being
black listed.
It twists our words
and warps our minds.

None are born with this sickness,
only infected later.
A fearful plague that pollutes
unwary minds.

Taught to hate skin.
Black should be white,
brown should be lighter
and the pink want to be orange.

What colors do you see?

Some will dispute,

annoyed at such talk.
Your privilege is annoyed.
The annoyance, your racism.

Of course they don't see color.
Everything is normal,
all washed out,
bleached.
They too were conned.
Sold their souls and
their spirits for comfort.
Culture lost to greed.
They blow dog whistles of Dixie,
offbeat and out of tune.

I see color.

We have hoodies of cotton,
theirs are white silk.
Ours cover our heads,
theirs their faces.
Our hoodies get us shot,
on streets we cross.
Their hoodies shield them
while burning the cross.

Their fires may burn bodies,
but the ignorance torches souls.
We sigh at another dumb comment,
ignore and try to make light.
We avoid the looks
as you pass on by,
your suspicions,
your disdain.
The guards turn a blind eye,

pretend not to see.
Shameful fragility.

They take our rhythm
but not our blues.
Shaking their hips
with no hops.
They want to forget,
ignore the Strange Fruit,
shun the Blackened Branch and
bypass the Blood Stained leaves.
The pain. The guilt.
It was never their fault,
but their silence is.

Privilege
to not see privilege
is the benefit of privilege.

The inmates cannot forget,
they live it.
They don't have the privilege
of forgetting.
The privilege
of not seeing.

Oh, I see color.

The terror of the first night.
They look at you different,
say you don't belong.
The venomous hate, the
baffling shame
of culture.

You tried to fit.
Tried to be like them.
Tightened your lips,
Lightened your skin,
Widened your eyes.
A mother's heartbreak.

You are not alone,
we are the majority.
The ways of the land are being lost
and traditions are vanishing,
but we will sing, we will dance.
We have centuries of stamina.

I see color.

They are lost.
They were misled.
They must find their way back.
They are good people,
They just forgot.

No opting out.
These chains are real.
Either you're watering or chopping
the gallows tree.
If you aren't battling racism,
you are supporting it.

But, they say 'it's over,
don't use the race card'.
What is over?
Break our backs,
callous our hands,
blister our feet.

All for color,
in the name of greed
and a personal museum.
That is privilege.
Take all the pieces
and then we play even?
Put people in prison,
then be angry when
they rattle cages.

Oh, I see color!
Child.

Your flawless skin
soaked by the sun.
The color of beauty,
a regal honor.
The crown of
history and culture.

I am not colorblind!

We don't need allies!
We need traitors!
Guards that expose the system.
To renounce the unholy treaty
that keeps them silent
for the sake of comfort.

The brave will stand.
Willing to face hurt,
willing to wash their dirt.
Remorse may tidy stains of guilt,
but integrity can only be laundered
through action.

Yes, I see color!

I see angelic black,
the reverent red,
the beautiful brown,
the courageous yellow
and the loving pink.
I see color to see history.
I see color to see story.
I see color to see them.
I see color, till
I see their true color.

Enough!

I refuse to believe that all
humans cannot live together
in peace.
For she held her bus seat for everyone
and he took a knee for all.
Let us comfort the oppressed
and oppress the comfortable.

The prison is broken.
Let it bleed.
Light up the grounds.
Rattle the cages.
This jail is breaking,
the backlash brewing.
Alarms and sirens wail.
Bustin' out dead or alive,
the freshness of freedom.

The black suited hombre shivers.
It was always about money.

Just money.
We see the game now.
We refuse to play.
It’s a monopoly.
The banker hoards;
stealing properties,
dividing lands,
segregating brothers.
Call the guards,
let’s break this board.
We’ve had the keys all along.
Grab the dice.
The card has been pulled.
Get out of jail...free.

Grandmother: Did you get the metaphor?
Girl: What?
Gm: Are you kidding? Monopoly.
G: What's that?
Gm: A game.
G: I have no idea what that is.
Gm: Oh jeez!
G: I'm not that old.
Gm: I may be getting old, but it beats the alternative.
G: Some of them say we should just let it go. That it's in the past.
Gm: Everything is connected to everything. The great web of life. Anything that is done or has been done has an effect on the entire web. Whatever we do to this web we do to ourselves. When all is connected how could we ever forget? We walk with the ancestors and sow seeds for the children. Our blood is one. We walk together, every step of the way.
G: Those kids at school say it's their opinion, that they can say what they want.
Gm: Any opinion that rejects another's humanity, violates their being, is not an opinion. It is violence!
G: But everyone's quiet. No one says anything to them.
Gm: Of course, bullies prey upon silence. It's terrifying. Most hope they won't be attacked next.
G: Yes, then they'll come after me.
Gm: They already have.
G: What?
Gm: They are taking your world.
G: Yah but how could I do anything?
Gm: You need courage.

COURAGE

All journeys begin with just one step.
For the great pilgrimages need courage.
Yet many of us take the paved road,
the comfort of a worn out avenue.

Our world is riddled with it,
discouraged followers.
Sheltered by comfort and dulled by luxury.
Most don’t go anywhere,
just on trips.
They haven’t seen a thing,
still don’t know where it is.

Why do you avoid what others avoid?
Want what others want.
How ridiculous!!

Courage or comfort?
The river of comfort is strong
and the winds will blow.
Rise and face the breeze.
Out of comfort, into courage.
It is a barren path to the grail.
Forge the trail!

If you are not leading you are following.

The dormant seed is
covered by darkness.
But shells will crack,
and come undone.
The insides are out,
nothing is hidden.

No turning back.
Don't cling to the warm soil,
reach for the light.

If you're not in the sun,
you will be in the shade.
Little grows in shade.

She lives in curiosity and
reaches for open spaces.
She competes with no one,
so none can compete with her.
For she is not dazed by praise nor
crushed by criticism.

Like a bamboo, stretch and rise.
Take massive action.
Reach for the heavens
or don't reach at all.

The rains will fall, the sun will scorch.
Soft and supple life will adapt,
hard and stiff life will expire.
A bamboo that bends
is stronger than an oak that resists.

Disappointment will come,
it preys upon will.
But discouragement is just an echo of
old defeats. Aftershocks of quakes
when your world was shaking.
It is not now, discouragement is old.
It is always old.

What couldn't you do
if you weren't discouraged?

What wouldn't you try?

What would stop you?
For even drops, tiny drops
will wear away a stone.

For within you is the light of
a million suns,
the shine of a thousand moons.
Keep reaching for that light,
the shadows will be left behind.

Out of the cave.
Out of comfort.
You're the one.
Stars have awaited your arrival.
The road is clear.
Do not throw stones before you.
Time to show up.
Take the step.
The shadows or the light?
The past or now?
Courage or comfort?
You choose.

Girl: Why u so harsh?

Grandmother: That was harsh? I'll show you harsh.

G: Ok, easy grandma.

Gm: What's harsh is you living a small life.

G: What do you mean?

Gm: When you don't live in your power and quietly accept a smaller version of your world, that is harsh!

G: I guess so.

Gm: Guess so?

G: I wish I was older. Then people would listen to me.

Gm: You cannot skip chapters, you cannot skim lines. This is your life, your story. We all have parts we don't read out loud, but you will live every word.

G: Sure.

Gm: Sure? We must smash those glass ceilings in your mind.

G: I have no idea what you're talking about. What does that even mean?

Gm: Child, are you listening?

G: I'm trying.

Gm: Listen. You must feel your power.

POWER

Chained and muzzled,
but they had forgotten,
you have claws.

At two you knew.
You knew your world.
You would fight for it.
You would cry for it.
You would roar 'mine'!

You expected more,
demanded more.

Born to fly
but taught to crawl.
For they broke you,
they had to.
They taught you tricks.
Trained the wild out of you.

Comforted by comfort,
rattles rattled,
and lullabies did lull.
Drifting off in the winter night,
you made a home of hibernation.

Trained to agree,
taught to submit.
Jumping hoops
for peanuts.

You have no power
because you believe you don't.

The cage is unlocked,
but you sit.

You obey your master.
Hide in your dungeon.
Make it your home.

But,
At two you knew.

Your hunger is aching,
morning is breaking.
Awake from the slumber,
look out your cave.

This is your domain.

No need to shout,
no need to flex.
You know who you are,
You are the lord of the country.

Like a god, beyond all limits,
roam wherever you please.
Free from all fear,
pound the earth with each step.
Stirring winds, deafening thunder.
Declare it again. Mine!!!

At two,
you knew.

All want to eat but few will hunt.
Hunt! It's better to be the hunter
than the hunted.

Show them what hell looks like.
From a tiny ember,
to a fire that will light the skies.
This is your world.
Expect the world.

Of course there will be letdowns.
Feel it. Let it break you.
Then like a breath,
let it in and
let it out.

Then go back to expecting.
Expect more.
Better to feel a thousand heartbreaks,
then bend to a smaller world.

This is your world.
The bear will no longer perform.
She rambles where she pleases.
No more hoops,
peanuts won't do.
She's done with the circus.

At Two you knew!

There are no limits for you.
Raise your essence.
Rise and rise.
Be the sun.

On your legs!
Reveal your claws.
Show your teeth.
Stake your claim.

This is your world...
You know what you want.
Go get it.

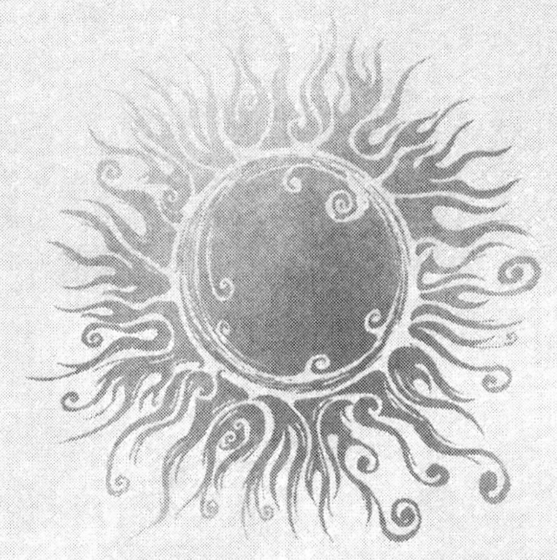

In my 18th year yes the immortal season of summer yes life is on fire and we are breaking free of rules and rooms leaving wastelands of watching clocks and staring at a box so we put on masks and come to the masquerade where we play men and women who bump into another and hold on yes curiosity bubbles yes apples are bit yes first dance first kiss first time yes in secret gardens we play where slow dances and holding hands mean everything yes love hurts yes our senses warmed and spirits run wild in our world and in our drama where hearts are shown yes we laugh like fools and love like poets yes sparks light the darkest part of our souls yes fires are stoked for we live in the embers and dance in the flames and we taste the fire of life while we shun the sun and howl at the moon for music is our sermon and concerts our church yes we sing in solidarity with fists and lighters in the air yes a thirst that can't be quenched yes hunger that won't be filled for we chew life to the bone and suck the marrow yes food nor rest is needed for we have friends yes the endless night yes one more song yes one more dance yes nothing to win and nothing to lose for the flames of desire burn in our souls while we reach for the highs and cling to the peaks for we don't know endings yes we never learned goodbyes but Stairway is playing the last dance we could hear the wind blow yes it was a lady we all know who shines white light and wants to show oh no how everything still turns to gold please no yet a new day will dawn and the stairway lies upon the whispering wind but my spirit is crying for leaving...for how to be a rock and not to roll.

Girl: Life is nuts!
Grandmother: What do you mean nut? Like peanut.
G: Funny. I just feel crazy.
Gm: Cus you are.
G: What?
Gm: Your life is crazy right now. You're playing with fire.
G: Just having fun.
Gm: Whatever you say peanut.
G: I do feel nuts.
Gm: I see you running and running.
G: Well, I gotta keep going.
Gm: You mean escape?
G: I never thought of it that way.
Gm: Well, you keep running from something.
G: Yah, I don't know but I'm having lots of fun.
Gm: Yes, until you stop.
G: Right. Then I feel awful.
Gm: You mean anxious.

ANXIETY

The hell of hell.

Shoulders will rise,
neck tightens, and
palms begin to sweat.
The guard is up and
the shields are down.

Where is the door?

This empty desert,
a Godforsaken place.
The gateway to
the devil and his angels.

The eyes hunt a haven,
but there is no shelter.
No shade, not even a cloud.

Where to run? Where to hide?
One foot here
One foot there
Leaving you nowhere

Mind is running.
World is spinning.
Hades is calling.

Can't see. Might pass out.
Heart races, breath bated.
the mind vacated.
Any minute now
Hell's gonna break loose.

Can’t breathe. Would rather die.
Just gotta get out of here.

The earth crumbles,
a bottomless pit.
I can’t go on,
I must go on.
I’m in hell.

Wanna run, but to where?
Wanna hide, but from what?
Wanna scream, but for who?

Where is that door?
Who could help?

They never came before,
what could they do now?
They are useless!!!
Am I crazy?
Gotta hide this.
I’m fine.
I can’t sit still.
My mind is killing me.
My chest is aching.
My hands shaking.
I hope they don’t notice.
Don’t worry about me,
I’m only dying.

Stop!!!
Illusions.
Delusions.

I hate this anxiety!

If I could erase it,
if I could destroy it,
if I could take it away,
I would.

But hear me.
This will not kill you,
it only fools you.
Makes you run from shadows
and hide in the dark.
For it isn't the strike but the
anticipation of it.
The guillotine is falling
but never cuts.
The snakes hiss
but never pounce.

Stop.
There is nowhere to run. Stop
Wherever you are. Stop
It is home. Stop
Stop just stop.

You need to rest. Everyone needs rest,
even you.
Of course you're exhausted,
it takes much energy to be anxious.
Anxiety does not ease the anguish of tomorrow
but will drain the energy of today.

Breathe.
It's gonna be okay.
It's gonna be alright.

You are not crazy.

You never were.
Your mind is good.
Nothing broken.
Nothing lost.

Just stop planning a crisis.
Nothing bad is happening,
and later on
nothing bad will be happening.
It's possible things will turn out
far better than you can imagine.

Just some feelings
between here and there.
Just some hurt
between here and there.
Sit in stillness.
In the spaces between.
Between breath,
between words,
between thoughts.
In the silence.

Breathe.

Don't run,
don't shun.
The dragon must be cooled
Avoiding her,
breath will quicken,
fires will rise.

Only one door and that is through.
When going through hell keep going.
Nothing is permanent, not even anxiety.

Breathe.
Feel it, don't fight it.
Believe me. No one is looking.
Don't be tangled in burdens.
The cure for hurt is in the hurt.
If you want to become straight,
let yourself be crooked.
If you want to become full,
let yourself be empty.
If you want harmony,
allow disharmony.

Go in to get out.
Feel to be freed.
The guard will crack, shiver
and move.
Shake and shake
till fright is afraid,
laugh it all the way
through.

No difference between anxiety
and excitement,
just a point of view.

A tourist of the ages.
Drifting in the past,
fretting the future.
Stuck in moments.
A time traveler
running from here
but never arriving there.

Come back here.
Be here and now.

What do you see?
What do you hear?
What can you smell?

Breathe.
Release the shoulders,
soften your forehead,
unclench your jaw and
let the tongue go limp.
Just breathe.
Drop.

Then dare to look again.
The skies are clearing.
Loosen your coat,
close your umbrella.

Breathe in slow
Breathe out slower
Breathe in slow
Breathe out drop
Slow
Drop

Nowhere to go
Nothing to do
No one to be

Breathe.

Peace
Peace
Peace

The doors unlocked.

The demons hushed.
You are home.
Smile.

Go slowly.

Girl: You make it sound easy.
Grandmother: It is. You've made it hard.
G: I never thought of it that way, but I know I'm always trying to get out.
Gm: Yes. You keep running from you.
G: It's been so many years of sitting. Sitting in desks, sitting at tables. I'm absolutely sick of sitting. I just want to move.
Gm: Yes, but don't let the remedy become your poison. Pace yourself, life is a marathon not a sprint.
G: Maybe it's easy for an old lady but I got stress.
Gm: Like having to party?
G: Yes!
Gm: Maybe that's a part of it. Too much drinking.
G: No.
Gm: Maybe. Well then quit.
G: No.
Gm: That was fast. Maybe you're addicted.
G: No.
Gm: That was a bit too fast.

ADDICTION

From the frenzied chase of joy
to the sublime bleed of addiction.

The chase is on.
The eyes
Chasing beauty.
The ears
Chasing sound.
The skin
Chasing touch.
A sense chasing nonsense.

Pick a card,
pick your poison?
It's Russian Roulette and
you're making bets
in a burning house.

She calls and calls
to the river she calls.
In your boredom,
from your tedium,
to your delerium...
she calls.
Come this once.

Just one last time.

One more time,
always one more time.
Turns and returns,
addictions feast on amnesia.

The slide of addictions.
Oh, the perilous ride.
You live for the action
and die for the deal.
The descent is
divine,
beautiful,
ecstasy.
A fool's paradise.

You run to the oasis,
but no thirst will be quenched
by a mirage.
For the slide
has sharp edges,
cuts with every turn.

Yes, just bleed me!
Take this boiling blood.
Take all of it.
Let me forgo today
till tomorrow.

Risk turned to reckless.

Under the gun,
you smell the smoke.
It's like fragrance from a flower.
The tambourine plays
while you fade
into your parade.
Oh, the glorious pain.
Echoes of the first rush.
Seeking the spin,
the one so wild,

you'll never spin again.

One more card.
One more round.
It's always one more.
Oh Jokerman,
you've played this hand.
It's a losing one.

All in!
Cut me. Split me open.
Just take it
Take it
Take it
Take it all
Anything for the slide.

Reckless to wreck.
Felt to felted.

Ahhh
The moment.
The one moment...
All is right.
I'm not here,
I'm not there.
No more pain,
No more hurt.
Nothing left.
Every wish,
every desire,
every dream
gone.
A fire doused.
Just ash.

Then quiet.
So quiet.
Bored.

The dark ash begins to rustle
The phoenix begins to rise.

Maybe one more time.
This time will be different.

But it never is,
never was,
never will be...
one more time.

The unquenchable thirst,
a ravenous hunger.
This mirage is the mistress
of seduction.
She'll deceive and tempt you,
but you cannot win.
Only the house wins.

Comfort to capitulation.
Risk to reckless.

The slide is waiting,
the ladder has no queue.
Up the rungs of hope for
one more ride.
Short cuts to heaven
and the devil is calling.
The doors open and the
music plays.

But here,
it takes more than two to tango.
Here we all run bad.
You bring all of us with you.
I bleed when you bleed.
I hurt when you hurt.
I see the demented dance.
It's been done to death.

If you must slide.
If you must bleed.
If you must one more time.
Walk to it.
Don't run.
Notice.

To quit hell,
You must know you're burning.

This is not easy.
Feel it.
Let it burn.

You will not stop tomorrow
for tomorrow never comes.
You can only stop now.
Not later. Only now!
Just now.
Just now.
Just now.
Stop before you start.

It's the dark side of the moon,
light some candles.
Close the backdoors.

From shadows to silhouettes,
you are not alone.
I am right here.

Reckless to risk.

But candles dim.
Rattles rattle.
Slides call.
Then it is just you...
Just you
In the dark.
Just you
In the silence.
Just you
And just you.
The devil will call
What shall you choose?

For the desert moon is bright.
She sees all.
But the devil is bored.
The dealer is dealing.
Ok.
Maybe...
one more time.

See you at the river.

Girl: I got the slide metaphor.
Grandmother: Congratulations.
G: Take it easy. I'm still young.
Gm: That's your fault.
G: What can I say I like to play.
Gm: Be wary of the rivers you choose. For currents will carry you until you become like the water that surrounds.
G: What?
Gm: Life is a balance. Do not chase highs, for every high has a slide.
G: What?
Gm: Too close to the sun, you'll be burned.
G: I get it. I get it. I'm just trying to be happy.
Gm: Happy? Ughh!
G: What's wrong with that?
Gm: That's all people ever talk about. This endless chase of happy. Do you even know what that is?
G: Um. Maybe. But I'm guessing you're going to tell me.
Gm: Good guess.

HAPPY

If your happiness has to do with reason.
If only reason earns it.
It will be lost.

The winds will blow,
reasons will whither.
What's here today,
will go tomorrow.
Will you still roll the dice,
gambling on a reason?
Is happiness chance or
is it choice?

Look at me.
I am old, but I'm content.
I have no reason, but
I smile at anything,
desire nothing,
love everything.
Simple as a fool.
Yet, I am happy.

Many will hunt happiness,
soaking sense and senses.
Just wounded vanity
and chasing after wind.

What they're seeking is joy.
But joy is a fleeting feeling.
Struck like a match and
gone with the wind.

Like parched men in deserts,

they grasp joy like water.
Squeezing the life out of it.
More and more and more
it feeds the seeds
of addiction.

Joy is not happiness.
Joy is just a feeling.
Another emotion like
anger or sadness.
Visitors to the soul,
phantoms of the heart.
Be a worthy host,
welcome your guests.
Entertain the shadows,
dance them into the night.
Then under the shining moon,
bid farewell.
For songs will end
and spirits must fly.

Happiness is much more
and much less.
It is right here and right now.
Ever since it heard your name
it has been calling you.

Come, let's sip from the sacred wine
of bliss.
The eyes will smile,
tongues will dance
and cheeks will flush.
Let's be drunk with delight
and high as the heavens.

Close your eyes,
just feel.

A summers breeze,
Novembers rain,
Winters hush,
Aprils green.
When the heart is free
it is the best season of life.

Relish the ordinary.
The moon at dawn.
The shores in yawn.
The sun at its peak.
The wind on your cheek.
Tilt your head back,
laugh with the sky.

Breathe in life.
Breathe out smile.
In life...
Out smile
In life...
Out smile
Simple.

No reason.
Just here, just now.
Just here, just now.
Not more, but less.
Having it all,
with nothing at all.

Drink will be magic,
food will be heaven.

Not waiting
for what the day will bring.
Just play through the light
and dance into the night.
Unabashedly falling in love
with all below and all above.

Happy beyond reason.
No cause, no excuse.

Not chance, just choice.
Simple...like a fool.

Sitting with a tiny smile.
As if all of life
is rigged in your favor.

This is happiness.

Girl: I get it. The outside world is always changing.
Grandmother: Yes. Winds will blow. Don't let weather dictate the day.
G: Weather?
Gm: You're kidding.
G: Don't cling to the outside world.
Gm: Yes.
G: It will always change.
Gm: Yes.
G: Drink as much as you like.
Gm: No!!
G: But I just don't feel right.
Gm: Our society feeds on you not feeling right.
G: What?
Gm: Well if you're happy you don't need much. Then you won't buy much.
G: You think so?
Gm: Why do you need to buy so many things? Cus you feel bad and want to fit in.
G: Well sometimes I don't look right. I don't feel right. Like I'm never enough.
Gm: Of course. You're a woman.
G: Ouch!
Gm: I'm serious. That's Sexism. That's how they get you. You feel bad enough, you'll buy anything to feel better.
G: Whoa, I'm not a feminist.
Gm: Why?
G: Well. Cus they're angry.
Gm: Shouldn't they be? Shouldn't you?
G: It's just not cool.
Gm: Ridiculous! Listen.

SEXISM

They labelled us lunatics,
claimed it was hysteria.

Laced with chains and
inspected by masters.
They check our teeth,
examine our hair,
judge our bodies.
No woman looks right.
No woman feels right.
No woman is right.

This is the insane asylum.

They always know,
always explain.
They start with a 'well'
and proceed with 'actually'.
They say it's lines not circles,
ladders not cycles.
That black is white.
That up is down.

How do they know everything?
Who taught them to know it all?

They are just confused,
smile at them and see.

Cat calls and dog whistles
from laughing hyenas to
jackals of misogyny.

We hear but won't listen.
We see but won't look.
We live the cycles.
We know rhythm.
We follow the moon.

But they shun flow,
discard cycles.

They were frightened,
locked us away.
They were frightened,
said we were not human.
They were frightened,
sold us like property.
They were frightened,
we burned at the stake...
They are frightened.

Their comfort
emits ignorance,
reeks of superiority.
They cloak their control.
The master
hides the chains.
The guard
denies the cage.
They say cuffs are gone
that we have the key.
That's a laugh!
We learned well.
For what they miss
we do to ourselves.

The masters seem out of reach.

So we blame each other.
Judge each other.
Hate each other.

Downright insanity.

Here femininity is blamed
and masculinity praised.
To succeed you must be a man,
to fail you must be a woman.
Nonsense!!!

It's time to step aside.
For in front of every great woman
stands a man.
Enough,
is enough,
is enough.

The asylum is crumbling,
the stones are falling.
It's weak, weary
and void of decency.

The witches have awoken,
we're beginning to brew.
The walls will be shaken,
we're beginning the coup.

Bang the plates,
shake the beds,
The asylum on the pyre,
patriarchy in smoke.
Stoke the fire, fan the flames.
We shall burn it to ash.

They took our plants
and gave us pills.
They brought us shame
and gave us clothes.
They hid the moon
and bowed to the sun.
Then raped the earth,
and stole their dominion.

Yet we belong to the earth.
She is not ours, we are hers.
She's waited and watched
while you dragged her down,
stripped her of her effects,
and hoarded her riches.

No more stories
Of how we are evil.
No more stories
Of mans greatness.
No more stories
Of what they deem equal.
No more stories.
No more stories.
Stop talking.
Just stop.

All together now.
Grab the trombone and blow.
All women shall rise.
Not proper,
not mannered.
Unbridled power.
No more masks,
no blessings in this disguise.

My body is mine and it does not forget.
I will not apologize for your chagrin.
I will not be pleasing,
I will not settle.

chains are melting
moon is calling
witches are brewing

Let's show them
True insanity.

Nothing to be afraid of,
You are ready.
For in your heart you know,
The most
Terrifying,
Powerful thing
In this asylum...

Is you.

Girl: It's getting better?
Grandmother: Yes, but we have a long way to go.
G: I just never feel like I'm enough.
Gm: You are and you always have been.
G: Yah, I guess all we want is equality. That isn't too much to ask.
Gm: Yes, but for the ones used to privilege, equality can feel like oppression.
G: The worst is, I just feel ugly.
Gm: If for a moment, you could see what I see, you would idolize yourself.
G: But a lot of times it's not men but women who pull me down.
Gm: Yes, it's internalized sexism. Did you hear my poem?
G: Yes, but it's long.
Gm: We blame each other instead of the oppression. We internalize the sexism.
G: Yah, girls can be so mean.
Gm: They are because they're hurt, it just comes out in distress.
G: Yah, but they are bullies.
Gm: Meanness is the disguise of weakness.
G: So what do we do?
Gm: Our only way back is to unite. To like each other once more.
G: Even them?
Gm: Yes, even them.
G: Why even bother?
Gm: I bother for the little girl you were, the woman you are and the old lady you will be. I bother for love.
G: Love?
G: Yes, a life without love is no life at all.
G: Oh no, here we go.

LOVE

Love is the bridge between you and everything.
There is no greater truth.

Love binds us. It is
Within us. It is
Without us. It is
Above. It is
Below. It is
All around. It is
the link. It is
the bridge.
It is.

Many bridges to the heart.
Some are long, some are strong.
Some are short, some are old.
The toll is all the same,
the cost is your guard.
The payment,
vulnerability.

Fortunate are the ones
who cross easy.
Hearts on their sleeve
and cards on the table,
they love others.

Fortunate are the ones
who hail others to cross.
Hands open
and arms stretched,
ready to recieve.

Some are loved
and find hard to love.
Some love
and find hard to be loved.

Rare is the one
where guards
on either side,
give easy pass.

All of us came with
willing hearts and
open hands.
But the winds blew
and bridges swayed.
Hearts were broken,
hands were closed.
The price we payed.

We learned caution,
learned to protect.
The watchmen was called,
doors were shut,
bridges were burned.

Yet in the heart a fire burns,
it longs and it yearns.
For deep in the palace,
the dragon stokes the coals
and fans the flames.

Surrender to the beast.
Be crushed by a crush.
The great river is roaring.
The winds are calling.

The horse called trust
is saddled.

This caravan of love
has many stops.
Burn all maps,
forget old trails.
Forge a new path
to the emperor.

The Great Bridge beckons.
A bridge so beautiful,
the eyes delight.
A bridge so becoming,
the heart flutters.
A bridge so tempting,
you may want to run.
The captain protects this bridge.
She shields the queen.
For this bridge is special.
One look and you shall never be free.

The sorcerer has arrived,
a spell has been cast.
The dragons hushed.
The dazed guards
lay down weapons,
raise a truce.

This love is not rational. It is not sane.
It is ungrounded, baseless, illogical,
absurd, unsound, absolutely foolish.
If you start with this, you're on track.
For love does not find the cautious,
only fools and drunkards are found.

Take the drink and soar to the stars.
Dance in your dreams and cry in your poetry.
Let the tears fall and the birds sing.
This heart was made to crack.
Be a hopeless fool.
For it is a sad man that has rationalized love.

But there is a lot of water under the bridge,
some other stuff too.
Every bird has a song.
Every cage has a door.
Every heart has an ache.
You may be caught off guard,
just cross.

Guards bow.
Hands open.
Masks removed.
Armor dropped.
Butterflies flutter.
Emperor is freed.
From her lonely wooden tower,
to be loved in the dark.

The eyes you've longed to see,
but even more to be seen.
Know his heart
For it is yours.
Know his soul
For it is yours.
Look deep into his eye...
It is you.
Care for this bridge,
it shall unveil many others.

For the guards will always
bow to the beloved.
A love so intoxicating
no water will quench it,
no dirt will smother it.
A bridge to the eminence.
Delight in the lust,
rest in the tenderness.
A dance,
you pray will last.
A dream,
you won't want to wake.

Yet, it is dark as it is light,
broken as it is holy.
The longing.
The hunger.
The poetic fire of love.
Just a look,
a touch.
Just feel it,
feel it all.
Let it hurt.
Let it break you.
Split you
into tiny pieces.
Sublime torment.
Shattered fragments
of a naked heart.

Feel I said feel just feel.
Break walls,
Build bridges.
Less guards,
More magic.

Cross.
Fall in love,
stay there.

In my 27th year, the descent of summer. The sun wanes, the fire to embers. The rivers of routine work their way deeper into our earth. They call it settling down. So we settle. The days duplicate and we replicate reruns. They are being engraved into our souls. Friends are pairing up and some marry. So we go to weddings and play dress up. Speeches are written and we begin to reminisce. We look at photos and recall days gone by. We are growing up. Friends are busy and circles become smaller. The nights spent in, the mornings we go out. We have bought in. We have jobs. We have bills. We are in the real world. We have left our bedrooms and sought homes. Thoughts are becoming worries and dreams are mortgaged. Now food is our refuge. This is where we gather. This is where we run. We trade dances for dinners, drinks for desserts. Pleasing palates while the fires fizzle. We live, but mostly watch. Movies are our stories and staying in our nights. Clocks are ticking and nests need filling. Some oblige and welcome the new ones. Others choose different. The road is split. Kids bring joy and also fatigue. The others don't know what they're missing, neither do the parents. We are trying to listen. Some understand, some just accept. They say it is time to ground, to return from the sun. No one to spite, nowhere to rebel. No need to fly the coop, the coop is now home.

Girl: Life has become full. So much on my mind.
Grandmother: About what?
G: About everything.
Gm: You are busy.
G: Yes, but I can't rest?
Gm: Your mind can't rest.
G: I have a lot to think about.
Gm: Yes. Many words. Many stories.
G: So much to figure out.
Gm: Maybe, but most of your thinking is a waste.
G: Well, I can't just forget it.
Gm: Well today is just the tomorrow you worried about yesterday. Did it help?
G: Maybe.
Gm: Worry is like my chair. It moves back and forth but goes nowhere.
G: Well...
Gm: Please. It's just worry.

WORRY

Thoughts, over and over.
Words, over and over.
Worry, over and over.
Just over and over and over.

Worry is quicksand.
Once you're in
you just keep sinking.
More struggle
More worry
More words
More worry
More thoughts
More worry.

This pit of wet sand
wraps around you,
sucking you into
a bottomless trough.

Stuck in the mucky rut.
Patterns around patterns.
Stories about stories.
Words above words.
Nothing more tiring than worry.

Stop it!
The more you struggle,
the more you sink.

Worry turns dips
into sinkholes
and gives small things

big shadows.

Just stop.
No more worry,
No more hurry.
Nature does not hurry
and all things are done.
Nature does not worry
and all is in accord.

There is sunshine
after rain.
There is laughter
after pain.

Nature has faith,
it trusts in trust.
Keep your faith firm.
If you have any faith
worry should be embarrassing.

For your hands do shake
as your faith does break.
Where you are looking,
is where you'll go.
What your eyes chase
the body will trace.
With breath too quick,
and the world too slow.

Your thoughts are leading,
be wary of the direction.
It keeps you running in the day
and swimming in the bed.
Breathe.

Don't mine for words.
Don't struggle.
The more you struggle
the more it'll pull you in.
Deep breath in...
then out.
Now yawn.
Yes yawn.
Let it all in.
Then let it out.
It is hard to yawn and worry.

The hands reach for the sun,
the jaw drops,
eardrums crack,
while breath
sinks to the earth.

Yawn.
A yawn inhales aimless wind
and
exhales a gentle breeze.

Letting go of words,
letting go of worry.

All worries begin with a word.
Go before the word, before thought.
Deep in the silence, in the darkest void,
is the seed of faith.
Close your eyes. Stay there.

More silence, less thoughts.
More harmony, less words.
More peace, less worry.

On your feet,
feel the dirt.
No more sinking,
just solid ground.

The mind has space
for worry or faith.
Choose wisely.

Girl: Yawning?
Grandmother: Yes.
G: That's it. That's all you got.
Gm: Child. That's all you need.
G: Sounds too simple.
Gm: It is. For each feeling, there is a release.
For sadness, it's crying.
For anger, it's shouting
For worry, it'syawning.
G: Well I gotta do something. I'm getting fat.
Gm: What?
G: The worry is making me eat.
Gm: Like apples and broccoli?
G: Funny. No!! Sugar, of course sugar.
Gm: Yes, the ambrosia of the Gods.
G: Yes! Cakes, pies, chocolate. Oh, god chocolate!
Gm: You mean anything that tastes good.
G: Yes! I tried to follow a diet but it didn't follow me back.
Gm: That's funny.
G: I'm so lost with what I should eat. They say this is good and that is bad. Carbs or fats I have no idea.
Gm: We eat food, not nutrients. It's become too complicated. Return to simple.

FOOD

Eat when hungry.
Drink when thirsty.
Simple, but vital.

They sold you a lie.
Eat this, eat that.
Told what to drink,
then how much to drink.
They indulged your desires and
coerced your cravings.

You used to listen.
You were hungry.
You sought nourishment,
sought connection.
The milk of life,
the love of mother.

Now it'sdifferent.
Food is a soother.
To cope,
to appease a crying babe.
Feeding your depression,
stuffing your anxiety.

Do you feel your hunger?
Does fire burn in the belly?
Or do you just distract,
crave a filler.
Stuffing yourself
with lifeless food.

When the stomach is empty, one problem

When the stomach is full, many problems.

There is a beauty in the emptiness.
When the mind and
stomach burn from hunger,
it clears the fog and lightens the world.
Fasting creates new habits, frees the mind.
It loosens the ties that bind us to material and
connects us to the spiritual. For a time each day
blind the body and see with your soul.

Then eating will be a ceremony,
a union with nature.
Food will be tasted and savored,
more than momentary pleasure.
Choose your food with
thought and care.
For those who gorge at buffets
don't know the taste of food like
the hungry do.

Eat like a bird, run like a horse.
Yet some will eat the bird,
and some may eat the horse.
Others may only eat plants, but
where does a plant end
and an animal begin?

Just eat with heart.
Food that has life.
Simple, cared for food,
unharmed.
For your being becomes your feed,
its history becomes yours.
Eat suffering become suffering.

Take time,
bite what you can chew.
One meal at a time.
Do not eat yourself out of
your senses.
Break bread with others.
There is enough food for all.
Feel the sun on each apple,
taste the wind on each kernel.
Saying grace with each bite.

The tongue has many customers.
The synergy of colors and
myriad of flavors.
Just don't be lost in one.
No flavor is worth losing oneself.
Too much spice will heat.
Too much salt builds fear.
Too much sweet creates worry.
But bitter in the diet,
no bitter in the heart.

With the simplest of food, you shall be one.
The union of life.
A genesis of beings.
The union of two is a sacred act,
treat it as such.

Take it all with a grain of salt.
Listen to your body.
Eat when hungry, drink when thirsty.
If you don't start with this.
All is lost.

Girl: I gotta lose weight.
Grandmother: Hold on. How did we get back to this?
G: I need to lose weight. I know I eat my feelings, but damn they taste good.
Gm: You know we could be talking about the end of the world and you'll bring up your weight.
G: Yah, but we are talking about food!
Gm: Ok. I'll give you that.
G: I'll never get a guy like this.
Gm: What are you talking about?!?
G: A guy, I need a guy.
Gm: You want a guy? I'll get you a thousand guys.
G: What does that even mean?
Gm: They're everywhere. Why do you need a guy?
G: Well. I think I need it.
Gm: You do not need it, but you could choose to be with another.
G: What about marriage?
Gm: Yes, what about it.
G: What good am I if I don't marry?
Gm: Oh dear. We've been told that since the beginning. Do you truly believe that?
G: No. Well, maybe.
Gm: Let me tell you about marriage.

MARRIAGE

The most cherished union,
the fusion of two.
The joining of families,
the eternal glue.

The rings of eternity in
sacred circles of love.
But stars follow an orbit,
and moons must become whole.
The five phases are essential for
for this ring to come full circle.

The first phase is new beginnings
The eyes seek beauty.
The hunter hunts.
A heart captured.
Words are a ruse,
the link is within.

The second phase is of the heart.
Dancing and spinning into the sun.
Twirling and whirling in the fire.
Two souls dissolving in the glow,
devoured by the inferno,
dying into love like tinder into flames.

The third phase is of your center.
The scent of the garden.
Be each others road home.
A window to each others heart.
Eyes of acceptance and hands of compassion,
the birth of a family.

The fourth phase is of the mind.
The winds blow many directions.
The candles are different
but the light is the same.
It may flicker, it may shade,
but the fragrance lingers.

The fifth phase is of the soul.
The waves of time pass.
Sitting in silence with
the soul of your soul.
The turn to eternity.
Love, laughter,
happily ever after.

The circle complete.
The moon is full,
the stars a glow.
From honeymoon
to harvest moon.
Nothing more sacred,
Nothing more whole.

Your spouse is your friend.
Your lover.
Your family.
Your teacher.
Your spirit.
Your home.

When you lose one,
you shall lose all.
But like a river finds the sea,
the heart can find its way home.

Loving will bring strength,
being loved brings courage.
But for every yin
there is a yang.
You may be the leaf
they will be the wind.
You may be the sea
they will be the shore.
You may be the rock
they will be the river.
For ones that are near often
collide.

Winds will blow and
trees will shake.
Waves will crash
and shores will break.
For here bridges are not drawn.
The windows are open and
the palace unlocked.
They have the key to the heart,
the map to the soul.

Of all the advice, one is universal.
To keep the peace, listen.
Just listen.
The little things are big things.
So feel, but watch words.
For words will be heard
and worse, remembered.
Keep it simple.
Not too much noise.
Listen.
That is enough.

Marriage is one conversation
that is much too short.
A friendship set to music.
Composed by the heart,
the divine dance of union.

It is a choicc.
A choice you make everyday.
To choose this person today,
to choose them for every day.
But choose someone who chooses you.
Who chooses you over and over.

The rituals of union, ceremonies of connection.
The circles sing, the rings remind.
Eternal knots are tied.
This is culture.
This is family.
This is marriage.

A true love story.

Girl: That simple?
Grandmother: Well, all marriages are happy. It's the living together that causes trouble. It's about having a good partner. We've made it complicated.
G: Where'd you meet grandpa?
Gm: At a wedding.
G: Whose?
Gm: Ours.
G: Really?
Gm: Never saw him till after it was done.
G: Wow, that's awful!
Gm: Is it? We were brought together by people who loved us dearly. We married into a family. I'm not sure I could have chosen better.
G: Really?
Gm: Look around. Who knows best? Are you so sure of what is best?
G: I can't even choose a boyfriend.
Gm: Right.
G: I would like to have children.
Gm: I'm glad that you're making a choice. These are all choices. If that is a decision you've made, great. If not, great.
G: But I heard it's a lot of work.
Gm: To have children is an offering, not a burden. You offer what was offered to you. An offering of life.
G: But how could I raise a child, when I feel like a child?
Gm: We're all children.

CHILDREN

It was a shipwreck,
the boats were burned.

We washed upon the shores.
The new people.
The new land.

We came in peace.
Warm hearts,
open hands.

Ours was the way of heart.
Our language, love.
We cried, we hollered, we laughed.
We were alive.
A land of milk and honey.

But milk spilt
and the honey dried.

They brought us here,
then pushed us away.
Said we had it wrong.
Primitive ways,
uncivilized.
We hid too little,
felt too much.

They covered our bodies
and taught us shame.
Soothered our mouths
and swaddled our souls.
Our spirits quelled,

while they forced
their way of reason.

Sat in desks,
locked in rooms.
We watched clocks,
wishing time away.
Dreaming of blue skies
under fluorescence.
Rows of obedience,
tests of conformity.

All lines.
Follow the line,
Write on the line,
Memorize lines,
Color in lines,
Stay in line.
We should have read
between the line.

They were feeding us facts
but starving our hearts.
Taught to memorize,
lines that hypnotize.
Taught what to think,
not how to think.

We learned to add but most
to divide.
Grades and worth,
who's better,
who's worse.
Is this on the test?
Always a test.

For the best hour of school
was lunch.
The best day was the first and
the last.

Teachers had good intentions.
Some took our hands,
freed our minds,
touched ourhearts.

But a colonist must colonize.
Factories need filling,
numbers need crunching.

It is sad but true,
to assimilate
is the breaking of you.

The home starts it.
The schools train it.
Work closes the deal.

They called it learning
and so we learned.
Steeped in conformity,
doused in civility.
Feelings for reason,
Eden for wasteland.
We danced for the master
and learned to please.
We took their language,
their customs,
their ways.

The greatest crime is the shame.

The shame you feel to feel.
The genocide of vulnerability.
Every time you go quiet.
Every time you hide.
Every time...
a piece of you fades.

Few survived,
often tormented.
Ones who still feel

Who paint
Who dance
Who love.

Yet, most are boats
without a rudder.
Watching the ships clock,
pretending to be busy.
Not here. Not there.
The ship has been leaking,
don't go down with it.

You never meant to be so
Obedient.
You never wanted to be so
Docile.
The ship's bell is ringing.
Go, you are old enough
to play again.

The revolution will begin at home.
The revolution is you and
your children.
The end of masters,

the liberation of slaves.
In the simple moments
where hearts are heard
and hands are held.
In the shadows of tears,
behind echoes of rage.

Don't worry about messing up
your children...
You already have.

They run wild and free but
thoroughbreds must break.
If you don't break them,
the world will.
The world breaks everyone.
If not, how would we ever mend.

Ours is to show the way home.
How to recover. How to heal.
To free the mind,
and be their best.
They may not listen,
but they are watching.
They follow what you do,
not what you say you do.

So many ways to feel bad.
What have I done?
I've screwed them up.
Am I good enough?
Am I doing enough?
Stop it.
You are good.
Start believing it.

Your kids will see.

Show simplicity,
their world is loud.
Show them slow,
their world is fast.
Show them breath,
their world is tangled.
Help them unravel,
undo what is being done.
Unwind what is being wound.

Each is different.
Ask about their dreams,
Listen to their hopes.
Learn who your child is.
Are they like a tree?
That reaches for the sky.
Are they like the sun?
The star of the show.
Are they like the soil?
Nourishing and giving.
Are they like the wind?
Aimlessly directed.
Are they like the river?
Steady and wise.
Learn who they are and raise them as such.
The greatest gift of life, is being who we are.

Hold your boys longer,
praise your girls more.
Speak to them like they are
the bravest, most beautiful,
kindest, intelligent and wisest
beings on the planet.

This will be the voice in their head.
The voice before words.
The seed of thoughts.

Their people know kindness,
they can teach you heart.
They are wise beyond what you know.
They live in fire.
Watch how they love,
see how they like.
Play with them,
dance with them,
run with them.
Hearts that are free,
far from shame.

All hands-on deck.
The wind is behind our sails.
The end of this oppression
will end all others.
Raise children to keep heart,
to keep their world.
Then they shall never settle,
for anything less
than absolute liberation.

The ship has come in,
the abolition has begun.
Remember who you were.
Your hands and heart open.
You loved life,
you liked people,
you were alive.

The land of milk and honey.
This is your domain.
You are the captain.
We came in different ships
but we're in the same boat now.
For this boat is not the
Mayflower or la Amistad,
Its name is freedom.

Girl: Wow.
Grandmother: Good, eh?
G: So long.
Gm: Oh please.
G: I just don't want to mess them up.
Gm: You will.
G: What?
Gm: But, you can show them the way back. It can also be fun. Oh, my Queen! You don't have to think about what you did, when you can lay back and enjoy it through your kids.
G: What?
Gm: Okay maybe I am old.
G: I miss those days of play.
Gm: Go play then.
G: Yah but with who? Friends are all busy. Don't have many friends now.
Gm: What?
G: It's just different now.
Gm: Friends are friends.

FRIENDSHIP

Red rover, red rover true friendship is never over.

The still of a moonlit night.
A lone wolfs unbridled cry.
But your pack is your pack,
be in the front they got your back.

This is your gang, your army.
Forever in stride.
Inseparable.
Untamable.

Your blood is one.
Friends will die for you,
Friends will live with you.

Eat like cows,
laugh like asses.
Breaking rules,
beating fools.
Free as the wind.
Whatever to whatever
to Anarchy.

The wolf will not join the circus,
this beast will not fetch.
So the pack won't follow clowns,
will not hide amid the sheep.

You have your own world.
You know these people,
you met at a different layer.

They will pull you up
when needed.
They will pull you down
when needed.

No one above,
no one below.
Side by side,
stride in stride.
If one fights, we all fight.

In this circle
the roles emerge.
The joker plays the fool.
The fighter will fight.
The writer will write.
The peacemaker makes peace
The philosopher speaks.
A balance forged.
A solid ring.

Remember who you are.
You have your own language.
Your own words.
Your own stories.
Your people.

They see your joy.
They sense your pain.
You can't fool them,
they know you're a fool.

Moments to memories
remind us of
who we are,

who we were,
who we always will be.

Our blood is one.
You are my pack.

If I don't see you
the pack is still the pack.

How could I lose you?
You're in my walk,
You're in my talk,
You're in everything I do.

You are my people.
You are my tribe.
If we don't see each other
that does not change our blood.
Our blood is one.
Our blood is forever.

We're still in the pack.

From pockets full of poesy,
we ran up clocks.
All black sheep
up those hills.
Twinkled with the stars,
sat on walls,
avoided falls.
But ashes to ashes
we all fall down.

Through all phases of the moon
we've played.

We grew together,
we shall fall together.

But the pack will still march.
No words needed,
nothing to declare.
For what could be said
We are the fools,
We are the pack.

Red rover red rover, we call you over.

Girl: We just don't see each other.
Grandmother: Yes, you're in different lives.
G: Yah, I don't understand their world.
Gm: They don't understand yours.
G: We were all together facing the same challenges.
Gm: You mean watching the same TV shows.
G: Yes. Exactly. Now we're in different worlds.
Gm: Yes, many more channels.
G: I don't want to lose them!
Gm: You mean your favorite shows?
G: Grandma!!!
Gm: Ok. Ok. Listen and you won't lose them. Have compassion.

COMPASSION

Compassion is the seed of love.
The soul of kindness.
The heart of harmony.
The grace of a god.

It's you I like.
It's not what you do
or things you can do.
It's not the way you act,
it's not how you react.
It's you, just you.
Cus I know you,
I understand you,
how could I not love you?

When we listen, we understand.
When we understand, we love.
Begin with listening,
begin with liking.
This is the birth of compassion.

Listen to the story,
but hear the storyteller.
Beyond story,
beyond thoughts.
For thoughts are
mere shadows of feelings
and stories just silhouettes
of sentiment.

Don't cheer them up,
take their hand and lean in.
We drop deep into story

to let go of the story.

Make it personal.
So personal
it becomes impersonal.

Hear with your heart,
listen with your soul.

The mask will drop.
The emperor freed.

Words to tears,
story to fears.

Words traded for sound.
Tales turned to sobs.

Stories discharged.
Storyteller incharge.

Your story is her story.
Your heart, her heart.

The freeing of souls.
The unity of minds.

This is compassion.

But we have feelings
and feelings of feelings.
Feelings of your feelings
and feelings of others feelings.

Feel your feelings,

empty the jug.
Only then can you hear others.

For compassion begins at home.
It starts with you.
The voice inside must be kind,
must know you're good.
Be compassionate.
To see others view, you must
be kind to yours.

See the dancer in the dance.
The story within the story.
For when you hear the story
you shall know the storyteller.
When you understand the teller,
there is no blame.
When you understand the teller,
there is no shame.

Your tongue is making you deaf.
Stop waiting to talk, listen.
Learn to speak, by listening.
Listening is kindness.
When the mouth is shut,
the heart can speak.

The more you listen,
the more you can reach.
But branches that reach too far
will be snapped by the wind.
Do not reach beyond your reach.
No more martyrs, no more sacrifice.
For what depletes you
will not benefit anyone.

Everyone hurts.
Nothing to fix,
nothing is broken.
Just listen.
Make long stories short.
More feelings, less words.
Listen I said listen just listen.

Offer your heart, give your hand.
Only an open heart can hear.
Only an open hand can be held.

All drops return to the ocean.
For seperation is a false notion.
Me and you is only a delusion.

The howl of the wind,
The crash of the waves,
The cries of the slaughterhouse.
Everyone and everything has a story.
Compassion is understanding.
Compassion is kindness.
Compassion is action.
Compassion is freeing all
beings from suffering.
If one suffers we all suffer.

There is no other.
We are each other.

Weep with the weeping
Roar with the roaring
Laugh with the laughing
You know suffering,
You know compassion.

Tell your story,
feel your feelings.
You shall understand all
if you understand yourself.
If you know this place
you know the world.

Walk with kindness and
proceed with grace.
Just listen,
just like.
Treat all with heart.
For compassion
is the highest form of evolution.

Listen up.
For the story is being told,
the storyteller is speaking.
But it is just one story,
it's about
Compassion.
And only one storyteller...
God.

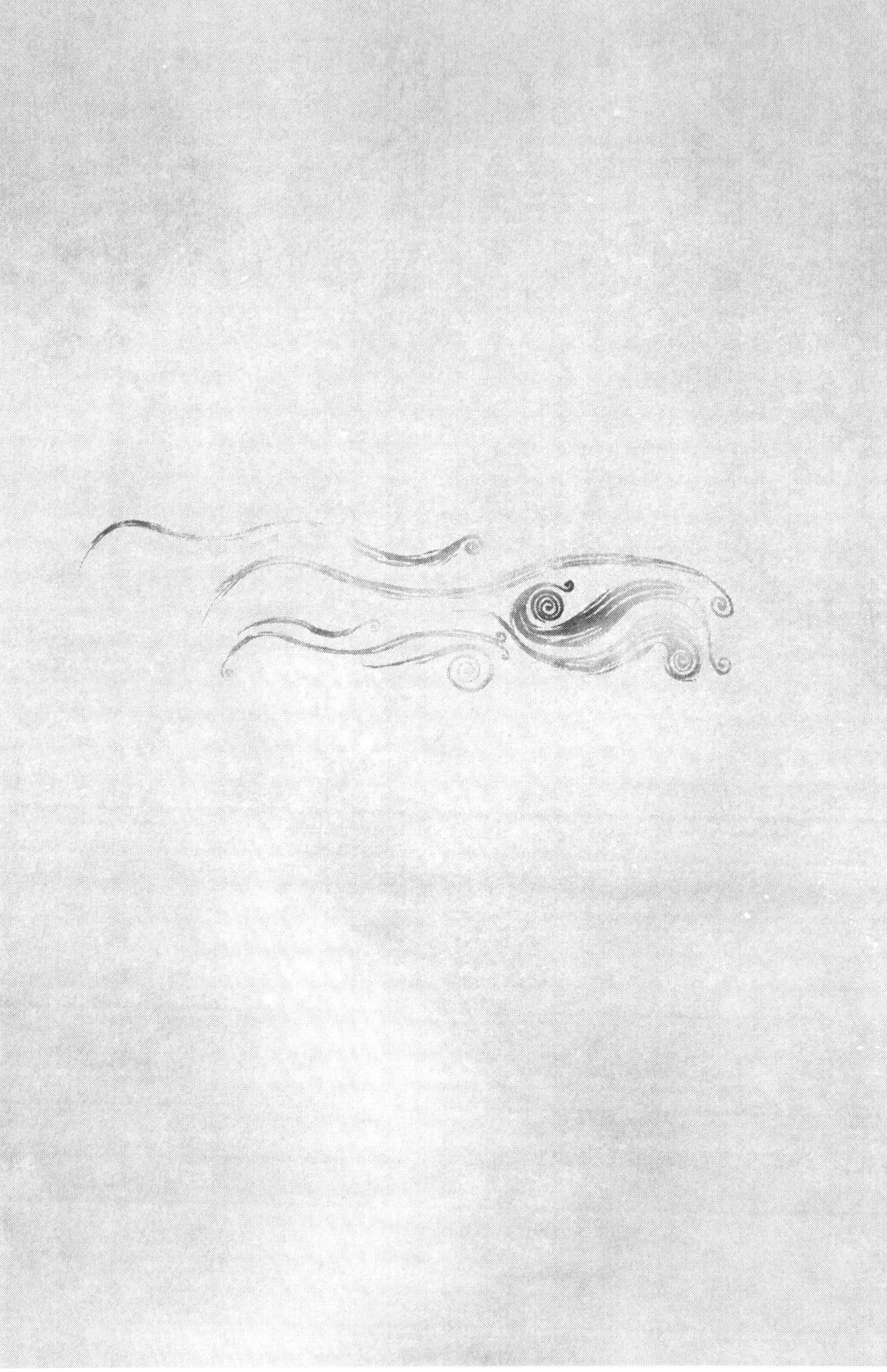

In my 37th year, the winds of autumn shake our foundations. Careers are stale and vows are breaking. The grief of silenced wishes and forgotten grails. It is the end of fairytales and happily ever after. No need to point fingers, for the dice was loaded from the start.
We wash our hands, call it new beginnings, but minds are messy and hearts cannot be reasoned. It is loss.
We are in the midst of reinventing our lives when grandpa dies. He is sick, he is old, we reconcile. Some turn to God, others turn away. Grief is having its way, chaos is the order.
The summer has given way to fall, the season of mist and ripened color. I have seen leaves turn my whole life but not seen them fall. They are falling.
The cool breeze is blowing and trees are swaying. The barricades can only hold for so long. Death uproots. Changes landscapes. Questions our truth.
We look for direction and seek reason. The heartache and the thousand natural shocks.
We question. To be or not? Some find answers clinging to the word. Preaching the way to comfort and salvation. Some brave the question and suffer the unknown. I am just lost.
For I have seen the sun rise but for the first time I am watching it set. My hands are open, my heart cracking. I have lived the springs, I am just now understanding falls. The beauty of the descent. The majesty of loss.

Grandmother just sat.

Grandmother: Child, come sit with me.
Girl: I have no time.
Gm: You are losing more than just time.
G: I'm ok.

GRIEF

You say you're ok...
So many times I've
heard you say this.

I know you're ok.
You learned to say that.
Nobody showed up,
in turn you gave up.

I don't want you to be
just okay.
It breaks my heart that you're
just okay.

What can you hold?
What can you keep?
Structures crumble and
buildings will fall.
All you have, one day
will be lost.
All you know,
will be unknown.

Are you ok with this?

We try to avoid loss,
hide from grief.
But in this kingdom of glass
nothing can stay hidden.
For in the heart of summer,
the winds of fall are calling.
In the midst of winter,
spring is rising.

We cling to peaks
but there is no summit
without a descent.
Without rain, no flowers.
Without death no birth.
Without grief, nojoy.
But we see loss as bad.
Gain as good.

Is that okay?

Do you truly know what is good?
Must you avoid hurt.
Must you run from loss.
There is no gain without some loss.
There is no loss without some gain.

Nature knows,
it honors all seasons.
It knows the rise and
it won't fear the descent.
She knows it is not personal.
The river may be an ace
while ladders
become snakes.

Grief cannot be bypassed,
for this life has many shades of blue.
It is the lease of love, the price
of a brave heart.
Avoidance only
hides us from goodbyes
and holds us from hellos.

Let it hurt.

For the only cure for grief is to grieve.
The rains will surge,
dams will break.
The taste of salt,
the sacredness of tears.

It may hit like a hurricane,
break you into pieces.
Let it break you.
Let it take you.

But all storms will blow away.
Then, after the apparent calm,
when it seems you're through,
it will come back in waves.
Just learn to swim.

But with each drop a loss of loss.
As the ego falls apart,
the heart falls into place.

I am okay with you not being okay.

A day without grief is a day without
awareness and compassion.
The heaviest rains will come
from the darkest clouds.
When it pours, let it pour.
Tears of grief
or tears of joy.
The rains clear clouds
and unveil rainbows.

We are all broken
...and that's okay.

Girl: I just feel empty.
Grandmother: At least you're feeling now. At least you're moving.
G: I may look like I'm moving, but I feel I'm standing still.
Gm: It isn't easy. It's a long journey to the self. It begins with a crack in the clouds. A thunderous call from the heavens. The rains fall to ease the weeping clouds and wash away trouble. I cry very easily. Sometimes a story or sometimes a summer breeze. I long for reasons to let the heart crack and play its song.
G: Just makes me question everything. Like what am I doing here? What's my purpose for being alive?
Gm: The answer is inside the question
G: What are you talking about?
Gm: What is your purpose?
G: I don't know. That's what I said.
Gm: Well. What do you want? What's your dream?
G: I have no idea.
Gm: As a child you used to dream.
G: Yah, I also wanted to be an armadillo.
Gm: Yes. Maybe someday.
G: I guess I did dream. That was long ago.
Gm: You cannot stop dreaming because the night ends, but will you live or sleep with your dreams?
G: What?
Gm: You're a sailor who's forgotten the sails and your dreams are blowing in the wind.
G: I have no idea what that means.
Gm: Neither do I. Just made it up.
G: Just feel pointless.
Gm: You are. There's no point. No direction. No aim. You are lacking purpose.

PURPOSE

Worth has a cost,
purpose is the price.

People chase joy,
but joy is like a drifting mist.
Little droplets falling aimlessly.

Purpose is the north star,
the compass to set our sails.
It clears direction,
sharpens clarity,
nourishes destiny.

To not only live
but to be determined
to live for something.
To serve a purpose.
To be of value.
We all need Direction.
We all need Intention.
The archer needs a target.

So where is your aim?
What is your target?

To know purpose
you must know passion.
What is your passion?

What do you want?

The great question.
Precious few will ask

and even less will answer.

You must want something.

I want you to want!
I want you to be hungry.
I want you to thirst.
A plant wants water.
A bird wants seed.
A lion wants flesh.

We are all created for some work.
Your spirit longs for it.
Your heart aches for it.
Be hungry.
All nature is hungry.

Your calling is calling.
Listen.

Smell the blood.
The heart thumps.
The eyes dart.
Nostrils flare.
The chase is on.

Save your prayers, hustle.
An insatiable hunger,
an unquenchable thirst.
With a fire in the belly,
and flames in your heart.

Like the archer,
take dead aim
and pull back the bow.

But!
Do not aim, unless
you are willing to hit the target.
Do not pull the bow unless
you're willing to succeed.
Make your second shot first.

Will you deny purpose,
sabotage victory?
The greatest insult to all of creation
is your timidity,
your doubt. No more hiding.
If your life is going softly,
you're living it too lightly.
Dream wildly.
If you want anything
you better make some noise.

What you choose, is what you choose.
Your purpose may be to sweep streets.
Then sweep.
Sweep with the fire of a dancer.
Sweep with the will of a bull.
Sweep as all of life depends on it.
Do it with heart or don't do it at all.

Mostly be proud! Love what you do.
Lose yourself in service.
Your work is either an offering or burden.
Where we offer, there is purpose.
Where there's no purpose, there is burden.

This is the great secret.
To receive, to truly receive,
we must offer.

For the yin needs the yang.
The night needs the day.
We must exhale to inhale.
So we must offer to receive.
This is the breath of the universe.
Simple.
If you truly want, then give.

Ignite the soul,
Strike hard.
Burn the midnight oil.
Burn like the sun.
Burn it all.

Erupt.
Like a bonfire
leave no trace of you.

Do not hurry, do not rest.
Don't leave it to maybe, make it a must.
Become one with your craft.
The great musician becomes the music,
the painter the painting,
the poet the poem.

Consumed by art,
they bleed purpose.

Let it absorb you, impair you, destroy you.
Let it kill you.
Let go of what is,
to become what might be.
For if you want the moon,
you cannot shun the dark.

You may sleep with dreams but
wake with purpose.
For the purpose of a life
is to live a life of purpose.

We are all called,
we are all worthy.
We all have value,
we all have purpose.
No money will quench this,
no joy could distract.

With all your force draw your bow.
Aim the arrow.
Still.
Hungry.

Go.

Girl: Yes, I need purpose, but what do I want?
Grandmother: You want what we all want.
G: A bigger house?
G: Seriously?
G: A joke.
Gm: What we all want is to have an effect. To be useful, to be of value.
G: Yes. Value.
Gm: The greatest joy is service. When you're in service,
you release you.
G: Lose me?
Gm: Yes, in the most beautiful way. Letting go of you, you become one with the world.
G: Ok, but where do I start? How can I live my dreams?
Gm: Dreams do not just appear. You cannot have crops without ploughing or cross an ocean without waves. There will be struggle. You must be willing to work. Start where you are. Start now.
G: Now?
Gm: Yes, I know one thing you do not wait to do, that's procrastinate. Start now, there is no other time.

BEAUTY AND ORDER

Put things in order.
Do it now.
Do it.
Act while it's still easy.

The winds haveblown.
Scattered peace is,
put things in order,
pick up the pieces.

Nature knows order.
The light follows dark,
spring follows winter,
rainbows follow rain.

The simplicity ofplacement.
A clear space.
A clear mind.
A clear heart.
All pieces back in harmony.

There is no beauty without order.
Start by discarding.
Learn to let go.
What can you hold?
What can you keep?
This is natures greatest lesson.

Start.
Start where you are.
The beginning is the most important part.

For you cannot have out

what is not within.
A messy mind,
a messy room.
A cluttered heart,
a cluttered home.

But do not hide from storms.
Do not cling to comforts.
Then any problem, is no problem.

The symphony will pause,
the cadence refrained.
Observe the silence.
The maestro knows the score.
It is not the notes
but
the space between
that
creates the music.

In emptiness, all is born.
For form is empty and empty is form.

The fields of possibility,
where painters paint and poets write.
It is the dance of Shiva,
the silence of Buddha,
the breath of God.

Create the space,
the fields are calling.

Get on top of it!
Procrastination robs you of time.
It makes simple things complex

and hard things harder.
Then you are lost to fate
and a slave of circumstance.
Only action pierces
procrastination.
Just act.
Tidy your house,
clean your closets,
wash your windows.
Light will only enter
where it's clear.

Leave everything
better than you found it.

Tidying is a sacrament,
a sacred ceremony
of purification.
For storms crack,
and mud will track.
Be pleased.
For if not for mess,
how would you find order.

The beauty of simplicity.
A clear path for the soul.
Open and empty.
For what is more pleasing than
an empty canvas.
For what is more beautiful than
a blank page.
Nothing more serene than a
quiet mind.
Silence.
Sacred.

The stillness before creation.

The grace of space,
in fields of possibility.

Girl: Are you trying to convince me to clean your room?
Grandmother: Yes.
G: I see you sit in prayer. Is that your sacred space?
Gm: Yes, and so is here and there and there.
G: Should I be religious?
Gm: Sit if you like. Believe if you like.
G: But what religion?
Gm: Same, same. Just different branches of the same tree.
G: Isn't it important to choose the right God?
Gm: No.
G: Yah, but some religions are just wrong. Some say evil.
Gm: Who is this some? They say a lot of dumb things. The problem isn't evil.
G: What?
Gm: The problem isn't that there is evil.
The problem is, that there is good.
We spurn hell, but heaven is the issue
For without heaven, hell would cease.
G: That's confusing.
Gm: What's confusing?
One does not exist without the other. Evil began with innocence. There is no cruel without kind. No bad without good. No hell without heaven.
G: Ok grandma this is getting deep.
Gm: When understanding is lost it is the birth of goodness.
The black and the white. The birth of morality. The seed of righteousness.
G: I guess with no good there is no bad.
Gm: Lost in duality. There's always a right and wrong. An up

or down. Good or bad. But how could a God of all things shun the left and cling to the right?

G: Right. God is harmony, but isn't there a natural good and bad.

Gm: In our language there is no synonym for evil.

No word for it. Then who is bad and who is good in the garden? Was it the snake or was it the voice? Are you so sure you know? If you haven't tasted a bad apple how would you know a good one?

G: Did god create us?

Gm: Maybe or maybe we created god. It's a fifty-fifty thing. Flip a coin.

G: I don't know how I feel about this?

Gm: Am I hurting your feelings?

G: A little. I believe in God.

Gm: You're hurting cus you're defending. That is why there's no conversation about anything anymore. You're not that fragile.

G: Ok. But I still believe in God.

Gm: Great. So, do I. But everyone's an atheist, minus one God.

G: What?

Gm: Well they don't believe any other stories except one.

G: I don't know about that.

Gm: Just stop defending. How could you ever hear and learn anything new if you're constantly shutting out different thought. Listen, then check within to see if it fits. Always check to see if it fits. If it does great. If not, throw it away. Your choice.

G: I just don't want to follow the wrong god.

Gm: There is no other god.

RELIGION

God is not religious.

Religion is constructed from location.
Faith is cultivated from region.

They translate the world
with myths of birth and death.
They are the narrators of nature.
the architects of the mind.
The makers of stories,
of stories that make us.

Yet,
myth was once religion,
till belief fell away.

How could one be right?
One area be right?
The chosen or the condemned?
It is a matter of view.
Which is the way?
Or is The Way the way?

There are many eyes that see the sun.
Countless ears that hear the wind.
Infinite ways to bow and embrace the ground.
Yet there is only one religion,
just many fingers pointing at the same moon.
But
God has no religion.
He came as a rebel,
sat with the broken,
fed the hungry,

suffered mans misery,
rattled the kings.

Then came the translators.

The story tellers.
Conveying the unconveyable.
Putting words to the wordless.
They shade the sun
and domesticate death.
They promise after life,
in exchange for this life.
Often rich with words,
scarce with actions.
At times inspired the best
and bore the worst.

Does it remind you of good?
Does it bring you to kindness?
Does it pull you to love?

Take notice.
From sin to cinnabar,
it isn't the religion but the effect.
It isn't the book but the reader.
The word may be clear,
but people aren't.

With God on their side,
they fight over books
left unread.
For the right looks for the wrong
as heroes seek an enemy.
But so much lost in translation.
Hell bent to be preached by the righteous,

heeded by sins and sinners,
and reveled by zealots.

They will fight for it.
Die for it.
Anything, but live for it.

But, God is not dead.
The heart of all religion is the same.
Just three sacred messages.

Simplicity

A lotus flower;

Epiphany,
Wordless,
Grace

Compassion

The cross;

Trust in trust,
Surrender to surrender,
Suffering to salvation

Patience

Aum;

The truth of truth,
The hum of the universe,
The sound of silence

Untranslatable.
No words needed,
no speech required.
Just understanding.

I want you to have the sun.
I want you to have the wind.
I want you to have god.

But where is God?

From the rivers of Babylon
to the roar of the Ganga,
God has no location.
For God is the whole circle,
whose center is everywhere
and boundary nowhere.

God is in the church,
in the prayer, in the word.
But god is all around,
it is the water we are the fish.
It is everything and everywhere.
It is all that can be seen
and what is left unseen.
Lucid.
It is what's left, when nothing's right.
It is what's right, when nothing's left.

Some give themselves to God.
But how can you give
what Is not yours.
For the house of God is your home.
The mountains her cathedral.
The wind her temple bells.

The choir her flowers.
The sun her shrine.
This is her world.
She is the host.
We are a guest.
We come when we can,
leave when we must.
Nothing is held,
nothing is kept.
Born with closed fists,
we die with open hands.

Be still. Slow the breath.
Breathe...

There she is.
You are not alone
You never have been.
You are loved.
She knows you,
she knows your goodness.
She will never forget,
even when you do.

My wounded beliefs,
Wisdom has healed.
My church is not built by men.
I don’t follow words,
don’t need translation.
My language, life.
My book, nature.
I believe the sun shall rise,
the winds will blow,
that waters will flow.
My religion is living.

Hallelujah

Let life be the chapel,
birds your church bells.
The hymns of God
in each step.
Praising beauty
in each breath.
Be the seeker,
hear the soul.
Like the sunflower to the sun,
follow the light.

Waheguru

So pray. Let itbe
the key of the morning,
the lock at night.
Become nothing and be
everything.
Sit with the Buddhists,
Spin with the Sufis,
Sing with the Sikhs.
Aum or amen
Salaam or shalom
God is all
God is everything.
Stand before the Lord.
See the sun,
Feel the wind.
Heed your karma,
Honor your kismet.
Bow to all. Despise none.
Nothing greater than
knowing your nothingness.

Myth or religion.
God is beyond speech and sound.
For her language is silence.
But translators will translate,
interpret and preach the word.
Listen if you like, but
you already know the language.

Girl: Are you an atheist?
Grandmother: No, no there's not enough holidays.
G: Well do you believe in God?
Gm: Yes, just don't trust the people who work for her.
G: Why do you keep calling God a her?
Gm: One day we're all going to learn what terrible scribes men truly are.
G: Then what's your belief or philosophy?
Gm: To seek. Philosophy is unanswered questions. Religion is answers you can't question.
G: But I want the truth. I don't want to follow the wrong path.
Gm: Did you hear anything I said?
G: Yes.
Gm: Be wary of the ones who say they know truth. They sell mirrors to the blind. The ones who know, don't know. They don't even know how much they don't know.
G: Do they lie?
Gm: Yes and they're not very fun.
G: What?
Gm: There's nothing funny in those books. Nothing at all. No laughs. God doesn't laugh?
G: Cus it's serious stuff.
Gm: Is it? What is so serious?
G: Well then, maybe everything is a lie.
Gm: Maybe. What do you think?
G: Then what's truth?

TRUTH

Truth?
Even their lies are lies.
Their deceit knows no bounds.

They said that you are no good.
That there is something wrong.
That you're bound to lose.
That you aren't enough.
You're too dumb,
You're too bad,
Too fat,
Too old,
Too young,
Too slim,
Too this,
Too that.
Lies!!!

All of their truth is one big lie.
They blind you with smoke
and insist there's no fire.
But they ignited the gaslight.
Fuelling your fears
by drowning your doubt.

Why do you believe such words?
Follow what others follow.
Do what others do.
Nonsense!!!

For Heaven's sake, stop believing!
No matter who said it,
or where you read it.

Belief is ridiculous.
Don't believe beliefs,
question them.
Question the unquestionable.
Belief is the death of reason.
Belief has no place
where truth is concerned.
The greatest wisdom is knowing
you know nothing.

The men on the chessboard think they know.
They cover sacred caverns while
they peddle faith.
Words weaker than vows made in wine.
They offer pills of comfort
and coax you to the river.
Yet the waters are crowded and cold,
for dead fish follow this stream.

Trained to follow, not think,
especially not feel.
Marinated in obedience.
Taught to put on masks,
to fit in, and above all
be serious.
But seriousness is the sickness.
Don't follow fools,
follow the rabbit.
Throw awaydisguises
be as mad as a Hatter.

Burn the sage and sages.
Purge the air of confusion.
Baptize. rinse, repeat.
Nature is the great teacher,

it unveils many truths,
For fire will cleanse the spirit,
water will wash the soul.

Peel away the entire onion,
the only thing to learn is unlearn.
For life has no name.
The solace of an empty mind,
the peace of a settled heart.
Let go of yourself.
No self, no problem.

Undress and dive into the stream of truth.
Wash away all that has been collected.
Then be left with nothing.
Just you.

Simple,
but people follow words,
stick to the script.
Here they preach words,
what cannot be put in words.
In the beginning was the word,
a word beyond a word.
Now poets anguish for a word
to express this word.
For no word has touched it
and no tongue has soiled it.
But the word was just a pointer.
When you know the direction
you can let go of the word.
Where is the one who
has let go of the word,
I'd like to have a word.

Pay attention.
Don't follow anything you hear.
Listen to what I say.
Chase the rabbits.
Take the trip.
It's your dream
You decide where it goes from here.

Be still.
Be simple.
Be truth.

In my forty fifth year. The days are shorter, darkness is settling in. Outside the snow is falling. Grandmother stares out her window. Over the years, she has seen many winters and this will be her last. How I wish the seasons would halt and the moon would stay. I sit with her. In the quiet. In the stillness. Silently praying for time to stop. She is my beacon, she is my light. I see her fire is dimming, her body breaking. She has used it fully. It is tired and ready for rest.

I listen for a change. A return to life. A sign that might bring hope, but her cage shakes and the bars quiver. It is the death rattle.

We sit and we sit, floating through the past. Waves of memories flooding the sands. We land on the endless shores for a mere glimpse. I ask everything about her life. I want to hear it all. Drain every last story from that beautiful mind. I can see the joy she feels roaming through the different fields of her time. I love how pleased she is. She has lived a full life, she knows it. She battled like a warrior, danced with devils, loved like a mother, all with the precision of an archer and dreams of a wizard. A wonderful masterpiece. A beautiful mandala. But in the end, nothing will be kept, the sweeper knows mandalas shall be swept. The clock is ticking. The sweeper is calling. I can't bear to listen. It is my hell. It is my heaven.

Grandmother: Why are you so quiet?
Girl: I don't know what to say.
Gm: Well. That's a first.
G: Funny.
Gm: Just spit it out.
G: Ok. Are you afraid?
Gm: Child...of course I am.

FEAR

If you're not afraid...
You will be.

The sea shall roar,
waves will crash.
We must move.
You can't cross oceans
by clinging to shores.

Run or life will run you.
A rabbit runs from the coyote.
A mouse from the snake.
They yearn to live,
so they run.

They are alive!

The dog will sit.
domesticated,
comforted,
tamed.
Eyes drooping,
ears dropping.

A fox is alive.
Ears pointed,
Eyes sharp.
Untamed,
hungry,
fierce.

Are you a dog or a fox?

Will you sit for your master
or will you run wild?

Fear keeps us alert,
keeps us alive.
Nature thrives in hunger
and dies in comfort.
But you see tigers
when it's only a cat.
You see snakes
when it's only a rope.

Stories creating illusions.
Stories creating delusions.
Stories creating fear.

An old fox knows the trap.

For it isn't waves that terrify,
it is the anticipation.
Fears of the mythical tsunami in
the silence before the storm.
Nightmares and terrors
on the frozen shores
as you brace for a crash.

You fear, fear.
Cling to your comforts.
You obey the master.
Trained to follow
for assurance.
Trained to heel
for refuge.

As a child you longed for light

and shook in the dark.
You prayed to the stars for shelter.
But now you sit in shadows
and hide from light.
Out of sound and
out of sight.

Forget this psuedo safety.
Stop your begging, the Universe
does not offer insurance.
It is not concerned of your fears
nor troubled by your angst.
The reassurance you seek
is only borrowed peace.
Any idea of security
is mere superstition.

So go where you
fear to go. Throw off the blanket.
Run into the dark.
The hounds are howling.
The moon is calling.

Out of the doghouse.
It is time to wake,
it is time to run.

Either you run from life
or run to life.You know what needs
to be done. Do it!
Life is risk!

Fear is meant to be felt
not followed.
Let it shake. Shake. Shake.

If you don't feel it, you will live it.
Break the chains of fear.
Run to it.
Scorn it.
Shatter it.

Do not let sleeping dogs lie,
put comfort to bed.
Amongst docile dogs,
be a fox.

Don't wait for fear
to come for you.
Go. Go into the dark.
Feel your light.
Standing tall,
Waves crashing
Yell!
'Come get me,
I've been waiting.'

Am I afraid?

Yes!
I am alive!

Girl: I am afraid.
Grandmother: Good. Feel it. It's life.
G: This life is just going too fast.
Gm: Yes, it slips away when you're busy living.
G: How did we get here?
Gm: How did we?
G: Just yesterday I sat on your lap.
Gm: Should we try it again?
G: Haha. No. It just seems the older I get, time goes quicker.
Gm: Yes, moments become memories in a blink.
G: Yes, and the more it goes, the more it takes away.
Gm: Time has a beautiful way of showing us what really matters.
G: It's slipping. I see it in the mirror.
Gm: Hmm. What do you see?
G: Time passing.
Gm: Your mind will follow your eyes. Where you look is where you shall go.

AGING

Mirror, mirror on the wall.
Where I look
is where I fall.

The years mapped on the face,
lines trace avenues of time.
The travelers eyes are tired and
the bags are packed. The hair scorched
with winter, while
embers left from old fires,
rarely fire again.

Where do you look?
The mirror will always show
what you're looking for.

All must age.
All cycles cycle.

The wheels turn in this
seamless orbit of time.
Every spring has a fall,
every day has a night.

But our fear of death
has lead us to scorn
the lines.
We long for the youth
and discard the old.

I have travelled far and found what
was near.
I made peace with the mirror.

We've declared a silent truce.
I swapped grey for silver,
wrinkles for laugh lines.
Aging has become wondrous.
A simmered sauce taste better,
an aged wine more full.

A good traveler is not fixated
on arriving.
For it takes time to stay childlike.
The more I've aged,
the more I like it here.
I enjoy the sights and sounds,
and sometimes
the mirror smiles.

But the looking glass won't lie,
I can see the passing of time.
I've worn a thousand faces but
the masquerade is over,
I've dropped the disguise.

The wind-swept lines,
creased over and over.
The same expressions rehearsed.
Mannerisms etched into
wrinkles.

I'm still learning to
break these patterns,
cross these lines.
I've learned years wrinkle skin but
rigidity wrinkles spirit.

For all will know death,

but few will know life.
I have seen many suns,
lived many moons.
Journeyed through many caves,
worn out many shoes.
I have learned where to step,
and when to stop.

Yet I'm still me.
The same me at 10 or 35 or 80.
How the years fell like rain.
I counted numbers till
I learned numbers don't count.

Smoke and mirrors.
Body a bit tired,
a bit shriveled.
A leaf drying. Nothing more.

Now my mind tends to forget,
at times it's a haze.
But I do not fear my forgetting.
It has little purchase on my soul.
I'm just more seasoned,
more at ease.
Why should I remember,
why should I recall?
It feels great forgetting.
Nothing behind,
everything ahead.
Don't pay much mind, the echoes have faded
for my sweet amnesia.

But mirrors do fog,
senses will haze.

I don't hear very well,
but I can listen.
My eyes are weak,
but I can see.
It's not dark,
but it's getting there.
It's quieter now,
the witnesses are gone.
I can hear the drops of rain.
Death is knocking.
The reaper is lurking.
He shakes the foundations
and rattles the walls.
Soon I'll be off the hook.
The mirror will crack.
The reflection in pieces.
Shards of broken time.

Until then it's tea in the mornings,
read in the evenings and
sit in the insanely quiet afternoon.
Just silent and still.
Nobody just me.
Everyone is elsewhere.
Doing.
I no longer do.
My doing is done.
I know the road has cleared,
don't know where I'm headed but
I'm well on my way.
One foot on the other side,
I'm just lightly here.
A shame,
for I'm just starting to understand.
Hear this.

I have lived!
Just live, love, learn.
Life passes in a blink.

Hold nothing back.
Then you are ready for death,
as a lion is ready for sleep,
after a good hunt.

Life is the mirror.
What you see out here
is what is within there.
Respect the mirror.
It cries with you,
it laughs with you.
It shows what you fear.
But most of all...
be kind to the mirror,
for
the one in the mirror,
may be listening.

Girl: Well that was heavy.

Grandmother: Don't bug me, I'm old.

G: I know, you're sick.

Gm: You're sick!

G: Ok easy. I was just talking about your illness. Is it hard to stay positive?

Gm: Positive?

G: Yes.

Gm: Oh you people are killing me with positivity. Surprise! I'm dying!!! Like I don't know this!

G: My yoga teacher says...

Gm: Aaaaah!!! No, please don't tell me what your yoga teacher says! Don't ever tell me what your yoga teacher says.

G: Well. Maybe you'd be more positive if you listened to her.

Gm: Your positivity is a pathology. Secret, I'll give you a secret. Stop avoiding life!

G: Ouch.

Gm: Buddha sat under a tree for 49 days. He lived the seasons and struggled through misery. He did not return and say life is great. No! He said life is suffering.

G: I don't want to suffer.

Gm: That's exactly it. The only way out of suffering is through suffering.

G: But grandma, she says if you want light, turn on the switch.

Gm: What the hell does that mean?

G: Positive mind. Positive vibes. Positive life.

Gm: Positivity? Why would I cling to such a feeble word? No, my child. Positivity is much too weak. It is for the ones who wish for the sun and hide from the rain. I do not hide. I play in downpours and kick puddles. Some avoid rain, others get a bit wet, I know I'm just soaked to the bone. When clouds break, I bathe in the sun. I live all seasons.

For what is positivity, but a cheap umbrella. How could you have rainbows when you hide from the rain. Let it rain. Let it drench you. Feel it. Feel it all. Then clouds will break, the sun will shine. True light. No lies. No concepts. Just fields of possibility.

G: But I like to stay positive. Have you not heard you attract what you are?

Gm: Tell that to the thousands of children who will die of hunger today. Positivity will not bring them food.

G: Grandma why are you so dark?

Gm: It's not dark it's truth. It's not negative nor is it positive. It just is. It cannot be true if it only applies to the privileged.

G: But, I just don't want to be negative all the time.

Gm: Listen. Your avoidance of suffering is the cause of your negativity. Suppressing, ignoring your feelings have created a slew of negativity in your body. Your fears, grief and anger that you push down will rise in your thoughts. This began long ago. They showed you a rattle to distract from your tears, from your hurt. Now you chase different rattles.

G: So feel it, don't follow it?

Gm: Yes, end this ancient habit of suppression. When you know darkness, no need to cling to light. No negativity, not clinging to positivity, just fields of possibility. Then you shall dance with the sun and be drunk with rays of gratitude. A life filled with purpose, happiness and peace.

G: But you are sick. There must be a solution. Something out there that can help.

ILLNESS

The ancients would say,
wherever you've been poisoned
the remedy is within fifty feet.

We all get bit
We all crack
We all break

But have you had enough?
Are you sick of your sickness?
Sick of your suffering?

We are all terminal.
Our time here is set.
The breath is bound,
the clock is wound.

But length is immaterial.
A mayfly lives a full day,
while the tortoise sleeps it away.

Health is the greatest possession.
The most sacred treasure.
Yet it is only cherished
when it begins to fade.
The knees get weak
and wills become meek.

We start to take notice.
Looking for shadows
and bumps in the night.
We see what we suspect
and hear what's not there.

We hope for comfort or a cure.
Maybe an elixir or a prayer.

Are you sick of this sickness?

We turn to the menders to sew our wounds.
For the needle longs for thread.
But some remedies worse than disease
and some cuts will not be stitched.

They came with good intentions by Apollo and Panacea.
With a poultice or potion to heal the sick.
But soon healers became the dealers,
peddling pills and doctoring disease.
Numbed into numbers, the dealer wants
you thinking that its either black or white.
But cures lose customers and labyrinths
have no exit.
For one pill leads to another and
mazes will not be remedied.

You are the author of your disease,
the scribe of your health.
It is better to maintain order
than to heal a disorder.
Just an ounce of prevention
is worth a pound of cure.
Curing a disease after it has appeared
is like digging a well because of thirst.

Your body has been speaking,
you just weren't listening.

Are you listening?

Are you sick of your sickness?

For you don't even know how good
this body can feel. The key to true health
is to care for this body inside and out.
For you could lose sight and survive.
You could lose hearing and survive.
You could lose your legs and survive.
But if you lose the air you will die.
You lose the waters you will die.
You lose the plants you will die.
Life is nature.
The elements are within you
and without you.
For what looms on the earth
will loom within its children.
Your body is your world.
We all share the same breath.
The forests are your lungs,
the sun your heart.

Of course there is disorder.
What can we expect
when we use water and air
as dumping grounds.
For the ones closest to land will know it first.
But we are all spun of the same web.
What affects one will affect all.
Their pollution will be yours.
Their hunger will be yours.

The rivers run dry
the earth scorched,
the winds whirl
and leaves turn over.
Nature shows signs before storms.

Learn the signs of nature,

if one element is in breach
the earth and body will suffer.

They only treat disease, not people.
Consuming climate, while saving gold.
Sacred oaths broken for gain.
Where assurance warrants insurance
and medicine aches for pain.

They add insult to injury,
chasing fires, smothering sparks.
It may bring comfort but
do not be fooled by blankets.
For sickness comes by horse
but departs on foot.

The fuel remains,
feeding infernos from below.
Listen for the sounds of disease,
the crackle of a twig,
the snap of a switch.
Act before the fire turns to flame.

Live with thought and conscience.
Not dying for a moments pleasure,
indulging in excess.
This causes energy to dissipate
and rivers to degenerate.
Learn restraint and know discipline.

Nothing broken.
Nothing lost.
The cosmic dance of energy and matter.
Move what is stagnant,
strengthen what is weak.

Harmony of yin and yang.
The balance of heaven and earth.
Not only to survive but thrive.

We all have a condition.
The only way to heal
is to know we're sick.
Be sick of this sickness!
What spirit forsakes
the body shall suffer.

Feel feelings.
Empty mind
Lighten body.

The coats preach fear.
The plants prescribe harmony.
To whom will you listen?

The disease is a call from
the moonless night.
Give yourself to the dark,
the dawn will come.
The remedy is near,
the cinder below.
Don't go without,
look within.

Girl: Well then find the remedy!
Grandmother: I have.
G: What?
Gm: I've looked deep within. Sat with my silence, listened to the gods. There is one medicine left. The only way out, the only remedy is to...
G: Don't say it.
Gm: Say what? You mean die!!!
G: Jeez. It's not funny.
Gm: Would you rather I just cry about it?
G: No.
Gm: Well I'm going to...
I'm going to weep that I'll be leaving you.
I'm going to yell Cus it's too soon.
I'm going to shiver Cus I am scared.
Then...
I'm going to laugh Cus it's all ridiculous.
G: I just want to spend all my time here. I know we're running out of time.

TIME

Just one problem,
you think you have time.

You are here,
not there.
For even there it can only be here
and back then it was always now.
Nowhere to get to,
nothing to get through.
Just here.

For time breeds
the illusion of then and there.
But when you look at that
you will miss this.
For the only way to that
is to notice this.

Don't let yesterday take up today.
Dreading the past and
fearing the future.
Your mind never on here.
Where you are,
what you're doing.

Truthfully there is no future, there is no past.
Just your imagination, just your memory.
Time is just space between moments,
yet there is only one moment.
Now.
The silver lining is here, on the golden sands.
For these are the endless shores of time.
Each grain sifted through the hourglass but

how could time be measured?
Time is not a few grains,
it is the whole beach.
At times you may carry the past
and may dread the future.
But the future is a thing of the past.
For even then and even there
you were here.
You were born here
and you shall die here.
Then you shall be here.
Here here hear.
Not there.

Once upon a time,
we looked to the sundial,
divided future from past.
From the shortest day
and the longest night,
we saw the cycles and
watched the stars.
Stones lined the circles of time.
Holding count with a silent chime.

Yet the unsetting sun has its own sweet time.
Nothing to get done or get through.
The sun never rises nor does it set.
It is only a view.

All clocks are circles.
All calendars cycle.
No beginning
and no end.
The past certain as the future,
and future fragile as the past.

Time never began
so how could it end.
For time is timeless.
Like tears in the rain.
The return of the turn.
The cosmic clock running
round and round.

Time is the great illusion.
Seducing you with seconds,
coaxing you with a clock.

All in good time.
No rush.
You have all the time in the world.
There is no such thing as busy if
you do one thing at a time.

The moon needs time to become full.
There is a time for it all.
The wanes and the gains.
For the rhythms of the universe
hold deep secrets.
There is cause to rest at dusk
and rise at dawn.
Live with tempo
and walk with pace.
In the morning act,
at noon mingle,
in the evening eat
and in the night sleep.

But time to time,
days will drag
and years will fly.

Hours pass but sixty
seconds relent.
For time is yours to spend
but you can't keep it.
Don't waste it, when it's gone
you can't get it back.

For we are only biding time at this shoreline.
Being swayed from zero to infinity.
The waves crash into moments,
and pull us into eternity.

Yet our suffering is simple.
It's being here
but wanting to be there.

Just be here.
Here, life is full of possibility.
Do not mourn for the past
and worry for the future..
When you are fully here
what is missing?
Not much.

Nowhere to go
Nothing to do
No one to be
No future
No past.
Out of time,
in no time.
You are here
Not there
For even there
You are here.

In life here
In death here
Just here.
The end of time.
It's about time.

Girl: I know what's coming.
Grandmother: What?
G: Not funny. This is serious.
Gm: Is it? New beginnings often look like painful endings. We've danced with wildflowers and sung with birds. We've watched clouds and savored the breeze. This is but another wind. Just another breeze. We sat together. We laughed together. We cried together. We are one.
G: But you will die soon
Gm: Yes, I will.
G: It's too soon.
Gm: I've outgrown my hunger. This is no place, without hunger.
G: I know.
Gm: Promise me one thing. You will speak of what we spoke. You will share what we shared. Carry the lantern so others may see.
G: I will.
Gm: I hate to leave. I truly cherish life. The world is a good place.
G: Can it be later? Just not now.
Gm: I wish it was so, but even later will someday be now.
G: I can't believe this is really happening.
Gm: I'm sorry child. Yet, I am a bit curious what's next.
G: I'm losing you.
Gm: We are branches of the same tree. How could I ever leave? Don't ever forget you'll always be in my hands and me in yours.
G: I must say all I can say. I must get it all in.
Gm: My dear. It will never be enough. It never is.

DEATH

What to say at the end?
What is left in the end?
A lightening flash
A blink of an eye
A wave of a hand.
How swiftly this life does pass
As we struggle through the pass.
For death does not wait
Fear of death our weary weight.
We've learned to avoid
Tremble at the void.
Ditch death and praise birth
But isn't death the birth of birth?
Without winter
No spring.
Without night
No morning.
For we all must sleep,
To awake.
Another drop back in the ocean,
Another wave in the ocean.
Ripples throughout time
Ripples of time
We look to the heavens,
Seeking heaven in the heavens.
For we learned to live,
But lost how to die.
Know death with every breath,
Not waiting the last breath.
But how can the wind die?
How can the river end?
How can the dust be dust?
For ashes to ashes, this is what we are.
Just to return to where we came.
For every dusk, there is a dawn.
Yet here the sun shall not set,

The moon only wanes.
For death is nothing at all,
an interlude,
an illusion of summer to fall.
Nothing bad,
Nothing broken.
All is well,
All is certain.
I'll always be here,
Though you might not hear.
I'll be the light of the morning.
The tears of your mourning.
As we turn toward the morning.
For in the freshness of the dew,
how could we bid Adieu?
A dance we've danced, over and over.
Many lives, over and over.
For what is ending?
Down the stream bending.
A dream never ending.
No time between here and there,
just feelings between here and there.
Yet as dawn gives way to day.
No green, nor gold can stay.
Rage, rage at the dying light.
Then...go gentle in that good night.
For that's how our world ends.
Not with a roar but a whisper.
The silent goodbye.
The solemn lullaby.
The lamp can be dimmed
for morning has broken.
Nothing is lost, do not hold breath,
Let tears flow. For grief. For love.
In our last breath we abandon death,
Freed hands from a worn-out glove.
A life well lived the heavens applaud.
Then bow, rest in the arms of God.

Now I sit in the chair my grandmother graced.
It's just quiet, so very quiet.
The ceremonies are done. People are gone. My mind longs for her refuge. My soul in pieces.
She said this day would come. But my ears would not hear, my heart could not embrace. I learned that seasons change and day becomes night but this, this could not be learned only suffered. It comes in waves and crashes my shores. I surrender and sink but there is no hand to hold. No voice to remind. No light to help me rise.
The rain of tears give way to a sprinkle.
It's just quiet. So, quiet...So I sit.
This is it.
This is what happens.
Outside her window kids play, horns are honked, life goes on.
I'm losing her every day. The softness of her voice. The sparkle of her eyes. The warmth of her touch. I hold tightly but time rips it slowly from my grasp. The memories fading into the dark.
So, I sit.
I sit in the chair my grandmother graced.
I sit like the old woman who understood comings and goings. She danced with the sun and whispered to the moon. She knew this was her world. She made that choice. She lit the stars and blew away the clouds. She sat with the creator and they created. She drafted her whole life. It was hers.
So now I sit.
I sit in this chair my grandmother graced.
It's my world...
I sit and I sit.
I remember her hands.
This cannot leave. The hands that held. The hands that touched. The hands that welcomed me home.
I open mine. I see her lines are my lines, her skin my skin. The crooked fingers leading to nowhere. The palms warmed by prayer.
I look to my hands and weep. That sneaky old woman. She was telling me this all along. How could she ever leave?
She is me...
So, I sit.
I sit in the chair my grandmother graced.

*

About the Author

Jag Johal is a Doctor of Traditional Chinese Medicine with over twenty years of clinical experience. He runs the Johal Health Centre - a successful and vibrant practice. Over the years he's helped hundreds of thousands of people reclaim their health through the Johal Method - a brilliant and effective protocol for optimum wellness that brings ease, joy and purpose to one's life.

Manufactured by Amazon.ca
Bolton, ON

21788201R00104